CRAIG L. BLOMBERG

Heart,

Soul, *and*

Money

A CHRISTIAN VIEW OF POSSESSIONS

College Press Publishing Company • Joplin, Missouri

Published in the USA by
College Press Publishing Co.
On the web at www.collegepress.com
Toll-free order line 1-800-289-3300

Cover design by Mark A. Cole

International Standard Book Number 0-89900-844-5

CONTENTS

Series Introduction 5

Study Introduction 7

1 Old Testament Law and History 11

2 Old Testament Wisdom and Prophecy 23

3 Additional Historical Background
    to the New Testament 35

4 The Teaching of Jesus 45

5 The Book of Acts 58

6 The Epistle of James 69

7 The Earlier Letters of Paul 80

8 The Later Letters of Paul 91

9 The Rest of the New Testament
    and Concluding Observations 101

2000 AND BEYOND STUDIES FOR SMALL GROUPS

In pursuit of our stated goal, "Every Christian a Bible Student," College Press has, since 1995, been publishing a series of *Studies for Small Groups*. These have proved very popular, both for group and individual study on a variety of topics and Scripture texts. Although, with the year 2000, we have changed the outward appearance of these study booklets, our commitment is still to providing solid, thought-provoking studies that will make a life-changing difference in the reader.

Of course, although we call these studies "for small groups," they are equally suited for individual study. If you are simply reading the book for your own benefit, please do take the time to use the "Reflecting on . . ." questions to focus your own thoughts. In a small group study, the questions should not only be used as a review, to see if you remember what was actually said in that lesson by the writer, but to help spark discussion of the further *implications* of the lesson material. Nor should you consider the questions that are provided the only questions to be asked. Any study is only as good as the effort you put into it, and the group leader should have read the lesson through thoroughly before the class meets, as well as encouraging all other members of the group to do so if possible. If the leader has gone through the lesson in advance, he or she will probably have thought of other questions, some of which may never have even occurred to the writer or editors of the study. After all, what is important is not just the bare facts of the lesson, but how they intersect with your own path in the Christian walk.

Above all, do not feel you have to race through the lessons. Although the number of lessons is purposely kept small so that no one has to commit in advance to an endless period of time on the study, you should not cut off discussion of an important issue just to fit the whole of the lesson into one study session. Nor do you want to leave off the end of a lesson because you didn't get it all in during the allotted time. The greatest advantage of the small group setting is the flexibility you have, allowing you to carry over discussion to the next session. Take full advantage of this flexibility.

HEART, SOUL, AND MONEY: A CHRISTIAN VIEW OF POSSESSIONS

More than a billion people out of earth's six billion inhabitants live in desperate poverty. Natural disasters, war, corrupt governments, lack of education, disease, unfair trade laws, and false religions all play their part in creating this situation. Conservatively, at least 200 million (one-fifth) of these poor are Bible-believing, born-again Christians.

In North America, trends over the last thirty years demonstrate an increasing disparity between rich and poor, irrespective of which political party has been in power at any given time. More and more, the growing gap between rich and poor follows racial lines: whites and Asians growing richer; blacks and Hispanics growing poorer.

Meanwhile middle- and upper-class Americans, including Christians, have markedly changed their spending patterns. We now eat out on average for nearly 30% of all our meals, compared to only 10% a mere twenty years ago. The amount of money spent on such nonessentials as sports and recreation, lawn care, video and computer games, home entertainment centers, pets and dieting has skyrocketed. At the same time Christians' per capita giving to charitable causes of all kinds has steadily declined in the last forty years from just under 4% of their total annual income to barely above 2%.

We are in the midst of the largest transfer of wealth in human history from the World War II generation to their children, the baby boomers. The possibilities of funding Christian ministry to address people's spiritual and physical needs at home and abroad are at an all-time high. But all the trends suggest that overall those inheriting this wealth are spending the vast majority of it on themselves, either to get out of all-time, global record levels of debt or to continue to fuel their self-centered interests.

Christian trend-watchers have made two staggering calculations. On the one hand, if every American Christian simply tithed, the additional amount of money that would be raised above and beyond current giving levels would be enough to eradicate world poverty in our lifetime. Of course, the sinful behavior of fallen humanity would prevent this from ever fully happening, but we could certainly make substantially greater progress than we currently are making. Second, the average age of major donors in both church and parachurch organizations is now, for the first time ever, well over sixty-five. Current Christian work is being funded largely by retired people, who lived a more frugal lifestyle a generation ago. Thus, unless patterns of Christian giving change dramatically, a majority of currently existing ministries will close their doors for lack of finances within one generation.

Astonishingly, while all this is happening, some Christian leaders are promoting a "health-wealth" gospel that pretends that it is God's desire for the already affluent Western Christian to become even richer. In striking contrast, every once in a while someone else seems to argue that well-to-do Christians should trade places with the poor. Both of these extremes prove unbiblical and probably discourage some of the rest of us from taking any action at all.

I have written this little book, therefore, because I have discovered that many Christians today are not willfully choosing to be disobedient to the Scriptures in the area of financial stewardship. They merely are unaware of the Bible's teaching on the topic and often unaware of the plight of the world and the kinds of trends I have just described. Many gladly increase their giving after a careful study of the Bible and current realities. Whether you are reading this book as an individual or as a part of a group, I hope that it can similarly encourage you to do more than you are currently doing. *Few of us cannot quite easily forgo certain expenditures in order to free up more money for the Lord's work.*

ACKNOWLEDGMENTS AND DEDICATION

This little book is the outgrowth of a larger study. In 1999, I published *Neither Poverty nor Riches: A Biblical Theology of Material Possessions* (Leicester, U.K.: Inter-Varsity Press; Grand Rapids: Eerdmans). As soon as it came out, I received numerous inquiries from students, pastors, and laypeople alike if a shorter and simpler version could be produced for people who did not want to go into the same amount of detail that I had. Several had in mind something that could be used for adult Sunday school classes or home Bible fellowships.

At about the same time, John Hunter of College Press and I were talking about the possibility of my writing for this "Studies for Small Groups" Series. I count it an answer to prayer that the publishers were so willing to go along with this topic as my suggestion for a contribution to a series of study guides that has already proved both popular and helpful. I am grateful for their support at every stage in the project. Because I have documented my material in great detail in my larger book, I have followed the pattern of some of the books in this series by not including end notes.

As I type this manuscript, it has been only a couple of months since my former pastor and seminary president, Dr. Clyde McDowell, passed away at the young age of 49 after battling brain cancer for just over a year. Clyde brought a renewed vision to Denver Seminary, where I teach, of wedding the church and the academy. He helped to establish a mentoring program in which all students would be in a spiritual formation group and part of a mentoring team. This involved a seminary professor, ministry professional, and layperson throughout the entire course of the student's studies to help their in-ministry training and experience. Stewardship was one of Clyde's passions as well: not merely of one's possessions but of one's time and talents, so that all of one's Christian life might truly come under Christ's lordship. It is to his life, ministry, and memory, therefore, that I dedicate this volume.

OLD TESTAMENT LAW AND HISTORY

In this lesson:

- ▶ The relationship of God, humankind, and the material world
- ▶ God's promise to supply sufficiently for everyone
- ▶ A person's responsibility to treat others fairly

THE LAW (GENESIS—DEUTERONOMY)

FROM EDEN TO SINAI

Permission for Productivity. The Scriptures begin with one of the most important principles about possessions in the Bible.

Like all of the rest of the material world, God created them as something good to be enjoyed by all humanity (Gen. 1:4,10,12, 18,21,25,31). Unique among his creation, humans were fashioned in God's image and called to be stewards of everything else God had created (vv. 26-28). That calling does not give us permission to be cruel to animals or to destroy the environment, but it does grant us authority over "animal, vegetable, and mineral" to mold and reshape creation in ways that make our lives more productive and rewarding.

> Humans were fashioned in God's image and called to be his stewards.

Redemption Delayed. Of course, the sinless perfection of the Garden of Eden did not last long. As part of their punishment for disobeying God, Adam and Eve were told that their relationships with other animals, plants, and the land would no longer be harmonious (3:14-15,17-19). All the rest of the Bible is about how God subsequently unfolded his plan to offer redemption to fallen humanity. Not until that process is complete and the new heavens and new earth described in Revelation 21-22 appear will any part of creation be fully restored to the *ideal* God originally intended for it (see esp. Rom. 8:19-22).

Generous Patriarchs. In Genesis 12:1-3, God chooses one man, Abraham, to be the ancestor of a chosen people through whom God will bless all the peoples of the earth, as he works out his plan of salvation. To those who will come to be known as Israelites he promises a unique, "promised land," the land of Canaan (vv. 5-7). Even though none of the patriarchs — Abraham, Isaac, Jacob, and Joseph — ever experiences the complete fulfillment of this promise, each lives in the land for part of his life and amasses enormous wealth. Early on in the Bible, then, we learn that it is possible to be both rich and obedient to God (20:14-16; 24:35; 26:13; 30:43; 47:27). At the same time, Genesis points out that the patriarchs are also generous in sharing their wealth with needier people around them (13:1-18; 14:20,23; 32:13-16; 41:57).

Prison to Provision. More than 400 years elapse and the Israelites are languishing as slaves in Egypt. God's deliverance of his people in the "exodus" demonstrates that he remains committed to their material and spiritual well being. He is ready to fulfill his promises of bringing them permanently into the Promised Land, but the Israelites' rebellion in the wilderness postpones that entry for forty years. During these years of wandering God miraculously supplies manna to feed his people in the desert. Exodus 16:16-18 describes the arrangements:

> Early on in the Bible we learn that it is possible to be both rich and obedient to God.

> Each one is to gather as much as he needs. . . . The Israelites did as they were told; some gathered much, some little. And when they measured it by the omer, he who gathered much did not have too much, and he who gathered little did not have too little. Each one gathered as much as he needed.

Centuries later, the apostle Paul would find timeless truths in these arrangements, as he would endorse these principles in his discussion of the collection for needy Christians in Jerusalem (2 Cor. 8:13-15).

FROM SINAI TO CANAAN

Timeless Principles. A significant portion of Genesis through Deuteronomy is devoted to the Law that God gave Moses at Mt.

Sinai for his people. Christians today do not literally follow every specific commandment of the Law because it has been fulfilled in Christ (Matt. 5:17; Rom. 10:4; Gal. 3:10; Heb. 8:13). At the same time, every passage of the Old Testament contains principles which at some level remain binding on believers in every time and place (2 Tim. 3:16). We must be sensitive to this balance in application as we focus on specific laws related to material possessions.

Two broad principles that complement each other may be immediately discerned. 1) On the one hand, *owning property* is a highly desirable goal that the Law attempts to make achievable for all God's people. 2) On the other hand, numerous *laws establish safeguards* so that people do not needlessly accumulate possessions at others' expense.

OWNING PROPERTY

Proportionate Property. Numbers 26:52-56 shows that God wants families and clans to receive parcels of land proportionate to their size. One of the Ten Commandments, the very heart of the Mosaic Law, prohibits stealing (Exod. 20:15,17). More specific laws concretely apply this principle. God's people must not move the boundary markers of personal property (Deut. 19:14; 27:17), use dishonest scales in weighing produce and merchandise for sale (Lev. 19:35-36), or accept bribes (Exod. 23:8; Deut. 16:19). These and similar laws stand behind the American ideal of every family being able to own at least a small piece of land, with a home and at least basic furnishings.

SAFEGUARDS AGAINST OWNING TOO MUCH PROPERTY

Loans and Interest. The number of laws that in one way or another relativize this ideal, however, outweigh those that promote the ownership of private property by about five-to-one. Perhaps the most surprising for modern readers are the laws against God's people loaning money to one another at interest (Exod. 22:25-27; Lev. 25:35-37; Deut. 23:19-20). While modern interpreters sometimes think that the Hebrew words used in these passages should be translated as merely prohibiting "excessive interest," Jews and Christians until the 1500s uniformly understood these texts to prohibit all charging of interest between fellow Israelites (and in the church age, between fellow Christians). But Deuteronomy 23:20 permitted the Israelites to charge interest on a loan offered to a *foreigner*.

As best we can tell, the only loans that were granted in ancient Israel were to help poor people. Thus it was wrong to make them pay back more than they borrowed if the whole purpose of the loan was to help them improve their lot in life. On the

> As best we can tell, the only loans granted in ancient Israel were to help poor people.

other hand, business transactions between people well enough off to pay back loans with interest occurred only as Israel traded with the foreign nations around her. Our modern banking and economic systems thus parallel this second situation more than the first. But legitimate modern applications of these laws probably do support the practice of certain Christians in certain parts of the world loaning to one another without requiring interest. When my family and I lived in Scotland, for example, it was common in Christian circles for various denominational organizations to grant interest-free loans to individual congregations for church-building projects. And, to the extent that Christians can influence international economics, we should probably support those efforts already under way in various countries to reduce or even write off the interest on debts that entire, desperately poor nations have accrued, that keep them from any realistic chance of economic improvement.

Periodic Limitations. The Sabbath, sabbatical year, and Jubilee all further prevented the uninterrupted accumulation of wealth in ancient Israel. God's people were unique among the surrounding nations in not being permitted to work one day out of seven. We often forget that this had an effect on their financial productivity. Once every seven years, the fields were to lie fallow, and debts were to be forgiven (Exod. 15:12-18; 21:1-11; 23:10-12; Deut. 15:1-18). Once every forty-nine years all property was to be returned to its original owners during a year of Jubilee (Leviticus 25). All of these laws were designed to prevent anyone from getting too poor or too rich.

> The Sabbath, sabbatical year, and Jubilee prevented the uninterrupted accumulation of wealth.

Interestingly, the Jews very faithfully kept the Sabbath but were very inconsistent in observing the Sabbatical year. It is debated whether they ever completely celebrated the Jubilee at all. This behavior demonstrates how radical God's laws proved, but it makes disobedience no more excusable. Again we cannot directly import God's ancient civil legislation with Israel into today's churches or governments. But Jesus will allude to the Jubilee in his famous sermon in the Nazareth synagogue (Luke 4:16-21), suggesting that the broader principle of concern to free people from their physical as well as spiritual slavery remains intact. Deeply embedded in the values of our founding fathers was the mandate, inscribed on the Liberty Bell that is still housed in Philadelphia, to "proclaim liberty throughout the land." Sadly, many today, even in Christian circles, who still cite this patriotic slogan, do not know that it is a direct quote from Leviticus 25:10 in a context designed to promote *economic* liberty and self-sustenance for all of God's people, however poor.

Tithing and Taxation. The laws of tithing and taxation clearly set limits on the amount of goods and money that Israelites could keep for themselves. By New Testament times, Jews had come to understand the "triple tithe" of Leviticus 27:30-33, Numbers 18:8-32, and Deuteronomy 14:22-29 as requiring them to pay back to the temple authorities 23⅓% of their annual income. In those eras in which Jews lived under foreign empires, including first-century Rome, additional taxes to the government often meant that godly Jews had to give up anywhere from 30-50% of their annual earnings or produce. And we sometimes complain of excessive taxation in modern America! We will comment further on the application of the tithe to Christians today when we come to Malachi in chapter two.

Justice for the Poor. Finally, we may mention various other laws concerned with justice for the poor. The laws of gleaning taught farmers to leave on the ground what was not collected on the first try at any harvest for poor people to pick up (Lev. 19:9-10; Deut. 24:19-22). A sliding scale was instituted that enabled poorer people to spend less than the rich on the sacrifices they offered for the forgiveness of their sins (Lev. 5:7,11; 12:8; 14:21-22). Deuteronomy 24:6 insisted that no court was allowed to take as collateral the garment in which a person slept, while Leviticus 19:15 and Exodus 23:3 required impartial justice more generally.

Fair Treatment of Foreigners. Numerous laws prohibited mistreatment of the foreigner or alien (e.g., Exod. 22:21; 23:9; Lev. 19:33-34). In many texts, the foreigner is grouped with the widow, the orphan, and the poor as classic examples of the marginalized whom God's people should help (e.g., Deut. 14:29; 16:11,14; 26:12-13). In an age when Americans, including Christians, debate how to treat illegal aliens in our country, it is interesting to note that there was no such thing as a legal alien in Israel. The land of Canaan had been uniquely promised to the Israelites; in that sense, all foreigners in the country were interlopers. Nevertheless, God commands his people to treat them with the same principles of justice and compassion as anyone else!

SUMMARY

At least four timeless principles emerge from this survey of the teaching about material possessions in Genesis through Deuteronomy. *First,* property is viewed as desirable, so that God's people should work to see that everyone has a fair chance at owning some. *Second,* we are expected to work hard and con- tribute our fair share, whenever it is humanly possible, to earn- ing our property and possessions. *Third,* those of us who suc- ceed at this more than others should voluntarily give up some of our possessions to help the less fortunate. *Fourth,* we should be concerned about public legislation and economic policies that discriminate against the poor. To the extent that we can influ- ence the public sector, we should work for principles of justice and compassion for every needy person.

THE HISTORICAL BOOKS (JOSHUA—ESTHER)

Obedience Rewards Leaders. One theme unites the subse- quent history of Israel. To the extent that God's people, and especially their leaders, were obedient to his commandments, God would reward them with peace and prosperity in the

Promised Land as they lived in freedom from their enemies. In Joshua, this obedience, with occasional glaring exceptions, enables them to defeat the Canaanites and possess the land. Judges reflects a downward spiral of increasing disobedience and Philistine oppression as punishment. The united monarchy under Saul, David, and Solomon leads to the golden age of Israel, as the country possesses more land and power than ever before in its history. Each of these three kings, however, sins in damaging ways, setting the stage for the divided monarchy: Judah in the south and Israel in the north. Only a handful of the kings of these two provinces, and then only in the south, prove faithful, so that ultimately Israel is deported into exile by Assyria and Judah is taken off to Babylon (Samuel, Kings, and Chronicles). Ezra, Nehemiah, and Esther all reflect the Persian period that comes next. Under the Persian ruler Cyrus, Jews are allowed to return to their land, rebuild their city, and try to do a better job of obeying God's Law.

Wealth Not Guaranteed. Not surprisingly, Christians who think that it is God's ideal for all believers to be rich regularly cite the arrangements God made with Israel during this period. What they fail to observe is that God made these arrangements with no other nation. Whereas the prophets can rebuke foreign nations for their injustice or mistreatment of the poor, demonstrating that the principles of the Mosaic Law apply at some level to all peoples, no other piece of geography is ever called a Promised Land. No other people are ever formed into a "theocracy," a country in which, even when there are human kings, God reigns and can overrule a king's command.

> No Christian is promised guaranteed material prosperity as the result of adequate obedience to Christ.

Interestingly, the New Testament repeats all of the broad principles that we find in the Old Testament with respect to poverty and wealth with one notable exception. No Christian is ever promised guaranteed material prosperity as the result of adequate obedience to Christ!

Sharing vs. Covetousness. As for principles from these books that do carry over to our day, it is important to note that even those blessed by God with wealth during Israel's tenure within the Promised Land regularly and generously share that wealth with the poor. Boaz in the little book of Ruth and Nehemiah after the return from exile (esp. Nehemiah 5) are two often neglected examples. By way of contrast, one of the sins that makes someone like Ahab so wicked is his endless covetousness, so that he has Naboth, a small landowner near his palace, murdered just so he can add that property to his already vast holdings (1 Kings 21).

CONCLUSION

Even in just one chapter we have learned that God created the material world completely good, but that humanity in its sin regularly abuses that world so that all of creation is now in a corrupted state. Laws, therefore, must be enacted to keep human greed and violence in check. God does not believe in pure *laissez-faire* economics. Sinful human beings, including Christians, will find ways to amass goods for themselves at the expense of the poor and needy of the world under *any* economic system. We must therefore recognize that all we have is on *loan* from God and that he calls us to be good stewards of all of it. There is such a thing as sinful surplus, when people accumulate unused or unusable goods while others languish as victims of impoverishing circumstances largely outside their control. Precisely because private property is a desirable good, we should work to see that everyone in the world has a fair shot at owning at least enough to live with some decency. Meanwhile, the Old Testament never sees one's material standard of living as an end in itself. It is always intertwined with the larger spiritual good of being rightly related to God.

Reflecting on Lesson One

1. In light of what you have read thus far, do you consider yourself poor, middle-class, or rich? Why? How do these labels affect how you seek to apply the principles of this chapter?

2. In what ways have you come to view material possessions as something inherently good or bad? What has led to your outlook? How should your perspective change, if at all, in light of this chapter?

3. What might applying the "manna principle" of not gathering too much or too little look like in the area of your personal finances? your family's? your church's?

4. Of the various principles discussed that come out of the Mosaic Law, which ones do Christians today need to work hardest at implementing? Why? What about you personally?

5. What is your attitude to personal property? How might it change if you were seriously convinced that 100% of it belongs to God and that he has merely loaned it to you?

6. Are there ways in which you have assumed that the amount of possessions you own was God's reward for your obedience to his laws? If this is not

a principle supportable by Scripture for Christians today, how can you better account for your level of wealth or poverty?

7. How much of your giving to the Lord's work goes directly to help the physically poor and needy of our world, including fellow Christians? What ways can you think of to improve your level of giving in this area?

Consider this:

The next lesson covers the books of wisdom and the prophets. During the period covered by these books (approximately 1,000 years) Israel, as might be expected, experienced a vast number of economic upturns and downturns. Each of us experiences similar cycles in our own lives. If you were told tomorrow that you were being let go from your job because of downsizing in the company, how would this affect your belief in God? Your time given to spiritual matters? Your dependence on God? Your giving to the church?

2

OLD TESTAMENT WISDOM AND PROPHECY

In this lesson:
- ▶ Keeping material possessions in perspective
- ▶ The value of wisdom
- ▶ The call to share with others
- ▶ Idolatry and wealth

THE BOOKS OF WISDOM (JOB—SONG OF SOLOMON)

JOB

Test of Faithfulness. One of the most well-known characters of the Old Testament is Job, who became enormously wealthy.

Then God allowed Satan to test him, and he lost his children, his property, and his health. The book of Job is primarily about how to understand and respond to suffering, but it has implications for how we view possessions as well. To begin with, it is possible to be extremely rich and still fear God (Job 1:1-3). In keeping with his unique covenant with Israel, God restores Job's wealth to him after he passes the test of faithfulness (42:12).

> It is possible to be extremely rich and still fear God.

Possessions in Perspective. But Job also knows that sometimes the wicked prosper and the righteous are impoverished (21:7-21; 24:1-12). So he keeps his possessions in proper perspective: "Naked I came from my mother's womb, and naked I shall depart. The Lord gave and the Lord has taken away; may the name of the Lord be praised" (1:21). Less well known is the fact that Job was always generous in sharing his possessions with the poor and often opposed injustice (29:12-17; 31:16-23). Thus he can declare, "If I have put my trust in gold or said to pure gold, 'You are my security,' if I have rejoiced over my great wealth, the fortune my hands had gained . . . so that my heart was secretly enticed . . . then these also would be sins to be judged, for I would have been unfaithful to God on high" (31:24-28).

PSALMS AND PROVERBS

Two major themes emerge in these lengthy books with respect to material possessions. Each must be kept in balance with the other. 1) On the one hand, we continue to read about the *unique arrangement of God with Israel:* as a nation, sufficient obedience to God's Law will result in national prosperity.

Thus at the individual level, personal faithfulness and industry often result in material blessing (e.g., Ps. 112; 128; Prov. 12:11; 13:21; 21:5). 2) On the other hand, more and more we read about the transience of this world's wealth and the *need for God's people to trust in him* no matter what their socioeconomic circumstances (e.g., Ps. 39:4-7; 52:7; Prov. 3:9-10; 23:4-5).

Dependence on God. So we begin to see a periodic equation between the poor and the pious, often represented by the Hebrew word *anawim* (e.g., Ps. 9:18; 68:5-6; 113:7-9). Not all poor people follow God and not all rich people deny him, but increasingly the Israelites experience what many other cultures have recognized throughout history: levels of religious commitment are consistently higher among the less well-to-do, who recognize they must depend on God for their well-being, than among the affluent, who think their buying power can meet all of their human needs.

Prosperity and Giving. The book of Proverbs continues to commend hard work as a key to earning enough to live on (Prov. 12:11; 14:23; 21:5; 27:23-24). Conversely, "a little sleep, a little slumber, a little folding of the hands to rest — and poverty will come on you like a bandit and scarcity like an armed man" (6:10-11). But those who succeed in attaining a measure of prosperity must again be generous in giving it back to the Lord and to the needy (3:9-10,27-28). "The righteous care about justice for the poor, but the wicked have no such concern" (29:7). For "if you shut your ears to the cry of the poor, you too will cry out and not be answered" (21:13).

Wealth and Divine Wisdom. Numerous proverbs compare and contrast earthly wealth with divine wisdom. "Choose my instruction instead of silver, knowledge rather than choice gold, for wisdom is more precious than rubies, and nothing you desire can compare with her" (8:10-11; cf. 3:13-16; 16:16; 22:1). So, too, "Better a little with the fear of the Lord than great wealth with turmoil. Better a meal of vegetables where there is love than a fattened calf with hatred" (15:16-17; cf. 16:8; 17:1; 19:1,22; 28:6).

Neither Poverty nor Riches. Of many other texts in Proverbs that we might cite, one stands out as somewhat different from the rest. Seeming to commend a "middle-class ideal," Agur in his collection of wise sayings in chapter 30 writes, ". . . give me neither poverty nor riches, but give me only my daily bread. Otherwise I may have too much and disown you and say, 'Who is the Lord?' Or I may become poor and steal, and so dishonour the name of my God" (vv. 8b-9)

> "Give me neither poverty nor riches, but give me only my daily bread."

At a time and place in which up to 80% of all the people in the land would have qualified as poor by ancient standards, seldom knowing if their trades or their crops would guarantee them enough income to feed themselves and their families, God calls people to be content if they know they have enough to get them through each day. In the biblical cultures only about fifteen percent of the population were ever reasonably assured of having enough reserve at any time that they could engage in longer-term planning beyond the season of the year in which they found themselves. These were the true "middle-class," and Agur is not speaking of them. A contemporary equivalent to his prayer might instead read, "let me be content if I know I am at least just above my country's poverty line"!

ECCLESIASTES AND SONG OF SOLOMON

Transience of Riches. If ever there were a treatise on the transience of riches, indeed of all merely human pleasures, Ecclesiastes is it (see esp. 5:8-17; 6:1-12). At a time when hope for life after death could not yet be based on God's fuller revelation in the New Testament, even the most fabulously wealthy recognized that they would soon die. None of their property would be of any value to them after that (9:11). But that does not turn this book into a call to renounce all material goods. Instead, one should enjoy them to whatever extent God chooses to bless one, fitting them into a context of dedicated service to God (see esp. 5:18-20; 11:19–12:1; 12:13).

Occasional Extravagance. The Song of Solomon primarily discusses the appropriate delights of sexual union within the context of a king's marriage to his beloved. But its picture of their lavish wedding (3:6-11) reminds us that once-in-a-lifetime ceremonies are often proper places for more extravagant expenditures. The question for many Americans, and especially Christians, today is whether the exception has become the norm.

SUMMARY

We may sum up the teaching of Job through Song of Solomon on materialism by again stressing that the Bible promotes no ascetic ideal. God does not call his people who have more than average amounts of this world's goods to trade places with the poor. But he does call on them to recognize how

God calls on his people to recognize what they have as surplus and to share from that surplus.

much they have that is truly surplus and to share from that surplus with those who have less than average.

THE PROPHETS (ISAIAH—MALACHI)

The final major division of the Old Testament in English brings us to some of the most "radical" teachings on possessions in all of Scripture. The prophets addressed the Israelites during the time of the divided monarchy beginning in the eighth century B.C., through the experience of exile to Assyria and Babylon (722-539 B.C.), and during the repatriation of God's people to their land up to about the mid-fifth century B.C. Because this entire period can be described as one in which Israel's pervasive sins finally led to punishment, followed by restoration in which the Law was better obeyed, we should not be surprised that the prophets focused on the ways in which the Israelites had disobeyed God and how they had to make amends. Five major themes emerge under each of these two prongs of the prophetic message.

ISRAEL'S SINS WITH RESPECT TO MATERIAL POSSESSIONS

First, Israel is worshiping idols made of costly materials. The prophets closely link riches with idolatry, in part because each pagan religion that influenced Israel made statues of their gods and goddesses out of gold, silver, and other precious stones (Isa. 2:7-8,20; 44:12-20; Hos. 2:8). But all the worship of false deities is wrong, whatever the financial price paid. And all allegiance to riches in place of God, even if not in the context of worshiping false gods, violates the first commandment of the Law — to have no other gods besides Yahweh.

Second, God's people are trusting in ritual rather than repentance. Jeremiah sarcastically mocks those Israelites who believe that attendance at worship in the temple and participation in its liturgy can save them from judgment while they oppress the alien, widow, and orphan in their midst (Jer. 7:4-7). We are reminded of Jesus' words in the Sermon on the Mount: "If you are offering your gift at the altar and there remember that your brother or sister has something against you, leave your gift there in front of the altar. First go and be reconciled to them; then come and offer your gift" (Matt. 5:23-24). If Christians today ever started seriously obeying this command, our churches would be temporarily emptied!

Third, the people are extorting, robbing, and oppressing to gain more land. Ezekiel 22:29, Micah 2:2, and Amos 5:11-12 all describe how the large landowners in Israel (already among the rich or middle-class) are trying to become even wealthier at the expense of the poor by forcing them into debt and into selling what little property they do have. Three specific practices that are sharply decried are the use of dishonest scales and prices in the marketplace (Ezek. 45:10-12; Hos. 12:7), foreclosing on unpaid debts (Amos 2:6-8), and defrauding workers of their wages (Mal. 3:5).

Fourth, the Israelites are boasting in their wealth. Amos contains some of the most biting and sarcastic rebukes of the well-to-do Israelites in all of Scripture. He lambasts those wealthy women, calling them "cows of Bashan," who "oppress the poor and crush the needy" and say to their husbands, "Bring us some drinks!" (4:1). He denounces the leading

> Amos contains some of the most biting and sarcastic rebukes of the well-to-do Israelites in all of Scripture.

men of the nation by exclaiming, "You lie on beds inlaid with ivory and lounge on your couches. You dine on choice lambs and fattened calves. You strum away on your harps like David and improvise on musical instruments. You drink wine by the bowlful and use the finest lotions, but you do not grieve over the ruin of Joseph" (6:4-6). Business in general has become so corrupt (Zech. 11:5) that Zechariah looks forward to a day when there will no longer be a merchant in the house of the Lord (14:21, see NIV note).

Finally, the leaders are motivated in ministry by their desire for financial prosperity. Micah 3:11 is representative of several texts that could be quoted here: Israel's "leaders judge for a bribe, her priests teach for a price, and her prophets tell fortunes for money. Yet they lean upon the Lord and say, 'Is not the Lord among us? No disaster will come upon us'" (cf. Mic. 7:3; Isa. 3:14-15; 10:1-2). The New Testament will make it clear that churches have the responsibility to take care of their full-time leaders' financial needs, but also that Christian leaders have the responsibility to forgo remuneration when it will send too many misleading signals in a certain context (1 Cor. 9:1-18). One wonders how many Christians have gone into ministry throughout our country's history because, among other things, it gave them a respectable job and income.

> How many have gone into ministry because, among other things, it gave them a respectable job and income?

WHAT ISRAEL MUST DO

First, the prophets call God's people to seek justice for the marginalized. Perhaps no prophetic text is more famous than

Micah 6:8: "He has showed you, O people, what is good. And what does the Lord require of you? To act justly and to love mercy and to walk humbly with your God." Equally important as background for Jesus' teaching are Isaiah 58:6-7 and 61:1 (quoted in Luke 4:16-21) and Ezekiel 18:5-9 (alluded to in Matt. 25:31-46).

Second, they must not boast in riches but be generous in giving them away. Here Malachi 3:8-10 is best known. The people are robbing God by not bringing their full tithes into the storehouses. Many people who otherwise do not believe that Jewish civil law carries over unchanged into the New Testament do think that Christians are still required to tithe. A brief study guide such as this is no place to go into the debate in detail. But it is interesting that those who still think tithes are mandatory normally do not insist on 23 ⅓% — 10% to go to the temple, 3 ⅓% to the poor, and 10% in celebration during festival time. Moreover, the synagogue is the Jewish counterpart to the Christian church, not the temple. Christians have no one central sanctuary in which they offer bloody sacrifices, which was the *one* function of the temple that set it apart from every other Jewish house of worship. Given the national averages noted in our introduction, tithing would actually be a substantial improvement for most Christians, but we will see when we come to Paul's teaching in 2 Corinthians 8-9 that it may still be too little!

Third, the Israelites are called to lament as a sign of their repentance. The entire book of Lamentations illustrates this as powerfully as any text. *Fourth*, Jeremiah 29:7 calls on them to seek the welfare of Babylon during their exile, a reminder that God can use his people even in situations in which they are an oppressed minority for the benefit of the pagan majority. *Finally*, they are to cling to the promises of restoration — the righteous remnant theme that runs through virtually every prophet's writing. Not only will Israel be restored to her land, as happens within Old Testament times, but she can look forward to a coming age when the entire earth is transformed, replete with luxurious material blessings (Isa. 54–55; 60–66; Ezek. 40–48).

CONCLUSION

In chapters one and two, we have just scratched the surface of the Old Testament's teaching on possessions. Because the New Testament teaching is more immediately applicable to Christians, and because there is a wealth of teaching on the topic in it, we will be focusing a greater amount of attention there. But before we leave the Old Testament, three summarizing remarks are in order. *First,* because of God's unique covenant with Israel, one cannot simply transport Old Testament teaching about prosperity as a reward for obedience into the New Testament age. *Second,* even within the Old Testament material goods are never ends in themselves but God's gifts in part to be redistributed by those with extra to those with less. *Third,* a key way of evaluating the faithfulness of any individual, church, or nation is to see how it cares for the poor and marginalized in its midst. These principles cut right across all the major modern economic systems and political platforms, making it impossible for the thinking Christian to endorse or condemn every aspect of either capitalism or socialism, either Republican or Democratic party agendas. Instead we must proceed case-by-case, issue-by-issue and see how the Bible addresses each debate in turn.

> A key way of evaluating faithfulness is to measure care for the poor and marginalized in our midst.

Reflecting on Lesson Two

1. In what ways has your income and net worth been a product of long, hard work? To what extent has it been dictated by sources outside of your control?

2. Give an example of how you have learned the lesson of Ecclesiastes about how fleeting the possessions of this world are.

3. Give an example of a joyful celebration in your life where you were not ashamed to spend more than you normally might have.

4. What are some contemporary examples of the poor who are victims of their own laziness? What about some who are victims of circumstances outside their control? Does Christian responsibility differ to these two categories of people?

5. What are some contemporary examples of rich people who are faithful Christians? How can you tell? What about some rich people today who have gained their wealth unjustly?

6. As you look at Israel's sins that the prophets denounced, what contemporary parallels can you discern, especially in seemingly Christian circles? What might repentance look like for us today?

Consider this:

Before reading lesson three, write a short description of what you think the world looked like economically in Jesus' day. After studying lesson three, compare what you wrote to the description by the author. How do the situations faced by poor, middle-class, and wealthy Jews in the year A.D. 20 compare to the lives of similarly placed people in 21st-century America?

3

ADDITIONAL HISTORICAL BACKGROUND TO THE NEW TESTAMENT

In this lesson:

▶ The economic environment of the New Testament period
▶ Glaring inequities between rich and poor

JEWISH BACKGROUNDS

Judaism continued to change during the four and one-half centuries between the end of the Old Testament and the beginning of the New. Persia eventually fell to Greece, which was succeeded by Rome. For about 100 years (164–63 B.C.) Israel lived as an independent nation, but the rest of the time she was under the domination of some foreign power. With each successive generation, Israel became more and more populated, with a once rurally based economy becoming increasingly urban. We have already alluded to the taxation that made life very difficult for the average farmer or fisherman, craftsman, or trader.

REPEATED OLD TESTAMENT THEMES

Jewish literature produced during the "intertestamental" period continues many of the themes that we see in the Old Testament. 1) On the one hand, Jews continue to assume that God's covenant arrangements are in place: sufficient obedience will lead to material prosperity. 2) On the other hand, the conviction introduced in the Psalms and the Prophets that the poor are often the pious rather than the rich grows even stronger. Commands to generous giving to the Lord and to the poor punctuate this literature as well. At times, almsgiving is described as the most meritorious deed a faithful Jew can perform. Hope for material prosperity for all in a coming age when the entire world would be re-created continued to grow as well.

THE ZEALOTS

By the first century, a tiny handful of Jewish and Roman landlords owned vast tracts of land in Palestine. Small landowners found it harder and harder to get by. Eventually many of them sold their property and went to work as hired hands of the rich, tilling the same land they once owned. When they were unable to pay their taxes, they took out loans and amassed debts on which they often had to default. In the most acute cases, some were thrown into debtors' prisons. Some even died there. Not surprisingly, by the 60s A.D., the Zealot movement gained enough support to try to lead a rebellion against Rome, in part because of the unjust economic system, even though the revolt was decisively squelched.

THE ESSENES

The Essene sect of the Jews, made particularly famous in the last half-century by the discovery of the Dead Sea Scrolls, took radical action with respect to property. At least at Qumran, the Essenes' monastic community on the shores of the Dead Sea, they created the concept of a "common pot" or treasury. Although it would appear from their writings that some individuals did retain certain private holdings, members generally had to surrender a large percentage of their personal property to the community who in turn doled it out, somewhat stingily, to people as its leaders saw fit. Food was raised and flocks were tended communally. Overall the members of the community referred to themselves as the "poor," building on the Old Testament concept of the *anawim* — the materially poor who were also spiritually dependent on God.

SADDUCEES AND PHARISEES

Among the Jewish leaders, Sadducees and priests (especially the high priests) often became part of the 2–5% of the nation who were enormously wealthy in comparison with everyone else. This came about in part because of their oversight of the temple treasury but in large measure due to their willingness to support and be supported by Herod's pro-Roman government. Pharisees and scribes were laymen, not nearly as powerful or

well-to-do, but still often among the small middle-class that was
at least one "cut" above the poor majority.

UPGRADING CLASS

Occasionally industrious workers among the "common people" could rise into this middle-class as well. For example, a city
in Galilee that has recently been excavated in great detail is
Sepphoris, about five miles from Nazareth. It was Herod Antipas'
capital in Galilee in the 20s and underwent a construction boom
during that period (as we learn from the Jewish historian
Josephus). Scholars debate how likely it is that Joseph and Jesus
might have benefited in their carpenters' work from the numerous jobs that were required just down the road. At any rate, we
cannot simply assume that the poverty of Joseph and Mary at the
time of Christ's birth (see Luke 2:24 in which they offer birds
rather than livestock — one of the Law's alternative provisions for
the very poor) continued without improvement during the next
thirty years.

JESUS AND HIS DISCIPLES

Middle-class. Similar hints suggest that at least some of Jesus'
twelve disciples were more middle-class than poor. Matthew's
tax collecting business probably vaulted him into this class,
though through ill-gotten gain if he resembled others
of his day. James and John, the sons of Zebedee, may
have come from one of the handful of more prosper-

Hints in the biblical text suggest that at least some of Jesus' twelve disciples were more middle-class than poor.

ous fishing businesses, because Mark 1:20 speaks of their family having "hired men." Even households with meager resources often had one servant, rescuing him or her from total indigence, but more than one "employee" in a household suggested some measure of prosperity. Judas Iscariot, perhaps the only disciple not from Galilee (Iscariot may come from the Hebrew *ish Kerioth* — "man of Kerioth," a town in Judea), may have been more well off than the rest, too. Judea in general was wealthier than Galilee, and Judas's role as treasurer for the disciples (and the greed that John 12:6 ascribes to him) may suggest some previous experience with large sums of money.

Keeping Property. Just as we ought not think of all twelve of the disciples and Jesus as uniformly poor, neither may we imagine them as having permanently divested themselves of all their property. True, Peter can declare, "We have left everything to follow you!" (Mark 10:28). But he will later lead a group of the disciples back to their fishing boats after the resurrection (John 21:3), demonstrating that they had not sold their property but merely left it for a time. Likewise when Jesus says, "The Son of Man has nowhere to lay his head" (Matt. 8:20), this does not mean that he is homeless. Mary still lived in Nazareth (Joseph may have died by this time), and Jesus himself seems to have had a house in Capernaum (Mark 2:1). Instead, Jesus is stressing his voluntarily chosen path of itinerant ministry.

Outside Support. Further insight into how Jesus and the twelve supported themselves comes from Luke 8:1-3, in which we read of several wealthy women who supported the little traveling troupe out of their personal means. A pair of apparently secret followers of Jesus who were also extremely rich were Joseph of Arimathea and Nicodemus (Matt. 27:57; John 19:38-40 — the amount of spices used to anoint Jesus' body came close to that used in the burial of kings). Thus when we read in 2 Corinthians 8:9 that "you know of the grace of our Lord Jesus Christ, that though he was rich, yet for our sakes he became poor, so that you through his poverty might become rich," we are not to understand literal poverty and riches to be in view. Christ in his incarnation gave up the incomprehensible privilege of sitting at the Father's right hand to be humiliated as a human and ultimately executed. That is how he became "poor." Similarly, we become rich in spiritual blessings, not necessarily earthly ones, as we become disciples of Christ.

> We become rich in spiritual blessings, not necessarily earthly ones, as we become disciples of Christ.

GRECO-ROMAN BACKGROUNDS

Welfare. While the Jewish synagogues and temple regularly took up collections to benefit their poor, the Greco-Roman world had no equivalent institutions. The Roman empire in general lacked any kind of welfare system, except for the "corn dole," established in 58 B.C. But this was limited to the city of Rome and to those who were its citizens and, in many cases, these were already among the better off, economically speaking. Greco-Roman ways of thinking often viewed poverty as the fault and just punishment of the poor. So it was very common for people to become disabled or diseased, homeless and helpless, with few if any people in the empire who cared.

Patronage. At the same time, the Greco-Roman world of the first century had developed elaborate forms of "patronage." Rich citizens of a community were expected to be benefactors or patrons. Much like in many places today, they gave generous donations for public works, religious buildings, music, drama, education, and so on. But they were also expected to have a group of less well-off townsmen with no year-round employment for whom they had a special obligation to care. The rich would provide odd jobs and at least enough of a stipend to live a marginal existence when no jobs were available, in return for which the poor "clients" of each patron were expected to offer civic support — to vote for their benefactor in elections, to acclaim him at public festivals, even to wake him up each morning at his estate, sometimes providing entertainment! Thus some of the poor people were cared for by the patronage system, but many, many fell through the cracks and were attended to by no one.

Philosophies. When one turns to the various Greek and Roman philosophical systems, other ideas emerge. Plato at times sounds like Proverbs 30:8-9 when he decries both extreme wealth and extreme poverty. The former leads to laziness and luxury; the latter to crime, he said. Plato preferred communal economic systems, while Aristotle promoted private property. Both agreed that the middle-class formed the real strength of a city. Zeno, the founder of the Stoics, taught

> Greco-Roman ways of thinking often viewed poverty as the fault and just punishment of the poor.

that wealth was a hindrance to wisdom. Epicurus, the founder of the Epicureans, is best known for his slogan, "Eat, drink and be merry, for tomorrow we may die." But Epicurus was no hedonist; he cultivated the "finer pleasures" in life — fine dining, choice wine, friendship, cultural activities — that which would avoid pain and promote what he believed to be true pleasure. The Cynics in some ways were the hippies of their world, deliberately flaunting conventional styles of hair and clothing with an unkempt appearance, begging for their keep, and at times engaging in immoral actions in public to shock the populace. Some of their practices resembled the voluntary, simple lifestyle of Jesus and his disciples (see esp. Matt. 10:8b-14), but the differences outweighed the similarities.

Elitism. Above all, the Roman empire created a two-tiered system in which the minority of residents who were actual citizens could generally hope to live a reasonably comfortable life, while almost everyone else was consigned to a lower socioeconomic bracket. In fact, the city of Rome in the first century was growing richer by the decade as the subjugated peoples from other parts of the empire worked harder and spent more to produce luxury goods for the elite in Italy. There are some sobering parallels with our contemporary world in which the Western nations continue to grow richer and most Third World countries poorer because of our ever-increasing craving for higher standards of living.

> There are some sobering parallels between the Roman Empire and the position of the Western nations in our contemporary world.

CONCLUSION

The Jewish backgrounds are more immediately relevant for understanding Jesus and his first followers. The Greco-Roman backgrounds come into play as the apostles move outside Israel with the gospel. Both, however, reflect widespread frustration with the economic disparities between rich and poor that increased in severity throughout the first century. Little wonder, then, that many Jews looked for a military Messiah who would help them overthrow Rome and re-establish an independent state of Israel in which they could revert to the more just laws and practices of their Scriptures. Many of them became disenchanted with Jesus, who claimed to be the Messiah but had little interest in political revolution. Little wonder, too, that many Greeks and Romans warmed to the apostles' message of equality in Christ across the wide, humanly created socioeconomic divides of their world.

Reflecting on Lesson Three

1. How does the historical background information in this chapter change the way you picture Jesus, his disciples, or any other characters on the pages of the New Testament?

2. What difference does it make if Jesus were poor or middle-class during his earthly life? His disciples?

3. Where today do you see parallels to the lifestyles of the Sadducees, Pharisees, or Essenes? Think about both the world and the church.

4. Who do you think has the primary responsibility for caring for the poor — the government, the church, wealthy individuals, or no one in particular?

5. What mechanisms today would best ensure that the truly neediest got the greatest amount of help that would benefit them the most in the long run?

6. Where today do you see parallels to the approaches described in the paragraph on Greek and Roman philosophical systems?

7. What do you think might have been the strengths and weaknesses of the patronage system? Do you see any similarities with any systems we have today?

Consider this:

In preparation for lesson four try to remember as many parables and other teachings of Jesus as possible. How many of these have to do with material possessions? Can you deduce one overall theme from these stories?

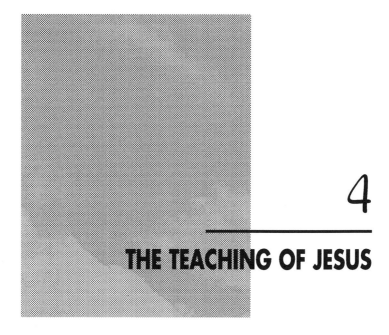

4

THE TEACHING OF JESUS

In this lesson:

▶ Jesus' teachings through parables regarding the handling of money
▶ Other teaching situations of Jesus regarding the handling of money

---

The heart of Jesus' message dealt with the kingdom of God. Jesus announced the arrival of God's kingly reign, even though God's political and economic promises to Israel were not literally being fulfilled. Jesus was most concerned that people become rightly related to God. But his "spiritual" message regularly had implications for how his followers used their finances. The most common form of Jesus' teaching involved parables, so we will look at them first. Then we will examine other important teachings in the Gospels that involve material possessions. In each section we will proceed through the life of Christ in chronological order, as best we can determine it.

PARABLES OF THE KINGDOM

FRUITFULNESS, TREASURE, AND COMPASSION

In the parable of the Sower one of the kinds of soil that proves unfruitful is that which is crowded with thorns and thistles. Jesus explains that the seed sown here corresponds to those who "hear the word; but the worries of this life, the deceitfulness of wealth, and the desires for other things come in and choke the word" (Mark 4:18-19). In the Hidden Treasure and Pearl of Great Price, he teaches that one must be prepared to give up whatever it takes, including material possessions, to enter the kingdom (Matt. 13:44-46; cf. the twin parables on counting the cost in Luke 14:28-33). In the Good Samaritan, compassion for the helpless victim across ethnic and racial lines is illustrated by open-ended financial help (Luke 10:34-35). And both the Friend at Midnight and Unjust Judge illustrate God's concern to answer prayer for assistance at both the spiritual and material levels (Luke 11:5-8; 18:1-8).

> God wants to answer prayer for assistance at both the spiritual and material levels.

THE INFLUENCE OF RICHES

Three parables teach particularly powerful truths about the influence riches can have for good or for evil. In the Rich Fool

(Luke 12:13-21), an inheritance dispute leads Jesus to warn about covetousness (vv. 13-15). Then he illustrates by telling the story of a farmer who had an unexpected bumper crop and had to build extra barns to store it all (vv. 16-20). Six times in the text, the man speaks about himself with the first-person pronoun "I." Never does he suggest that any of this surplus ought to help the needy who, as we have seen in previous chapters, would have constituted about 80% of the peasants and villagers surrounding him. Suddenly, his life comes to an end and he can't take his riches with him. Jesus concluded, "This is how it will be with those who store up things for themselves but are not rich toward God" (v. 21).

SHREWDNESS AND FAITHFULNESS

In the Unjust Steward, Jesus praises a man for his shrewdness in devising a way to ingratiate himself to his masters' debtors so that they will owe him a favor after he has been fired from his job (Luke 16:1-8a). Jesus then ironically laments that those who are not God's people are often shrewder in their dealings with the things and people of this world than are believers (v. 8b). He thus calls his disciples to imitate the shrewdness (not the injustice!) of the steward with this world's wealth. As they use possessions for kingdom purposes — bringing men and women to Christ, nurturing them in the faith, and caring for their various needs — those who die and precede us to heaven will thankfully welcome us when we eventually join them (v. 9). Faithfulness in the stewardship of material possession has a direct bearing on the amount of trust God will give us with spiritual treasure

> Faithfulness with material possessions has a direct bearing on the amount of trust God will give us with spiritual treasure.

(vv. 10-12), since one can give ultimate allegiance only to one of the two, not to both (v. 13).

REWARDS OF INDIFFERENCE

In the story of the Rich Man and Lazarus (Luke 16:19-31), Jesus returns to the potentially damning power of wealth. Here is a man who daily feasts as only the very rich could in his day but ignores a diseased beggar at his doorstep, refusing to provide even the leftovers for his nourishment. We get a clue in verse 30 that the rich man was not right with God when he begs Abraham to send Lazarus back from the underworld to warn his still living brothers to repent. In asking for this, the man as much as admits that he himself had never repented. But the only way that the story illustrates this lack of relationship with God is by his unrelentingly selfish use of his wealth.

RETURNS ON INVESTMENTS

The parable of the Pounds (Luke 19:11-27; cf. the Talents in Matt. 25:14-30) teaches about the need for Christ's followers to put the gifts he gives them to good use. While Jesus is not talking just about material goods, these are included within our stewardship. Comparing the

> The one who refuses to do anything with what he or she has been given is condemned outright as no true disciple.

Pounds and the Talents demonstrates that God's people are variously gifted and that stewardship results in various yields. The kind of person who is condemned outright is the one who refuses to do anything with what he or she has been given. Such a person is no true disciple.

WHO'S IN OR OUT

In the Wedding Banquet (Matt. 22:1-14; cf. the Great Supper in Luke 14:16-24), God's concern for the outcast and dispossessed of the land appears clearly. Although numerous details differ between the two parables, both include the striking contrast between many who think they are God's people, yet are declared to be outside the kingdom, and many whom the orthodox Jew in Jesus' day would have stigmatized as second-class citizens who nevertheless find their way in. Finally, whether one understands Christ's "brothers" in Matthew 25:40 to mean "anyone in need" (a popular view today) or "itinerant Christian missionaries" (the more common view throughout the history of the church), the story of the Sheep and the Goats clearly demonstrates that one of the marks of the true disciple will be to care for the physical needs of some of the most hurting people in our world today (25:31-46).

> The true disciple will care for the physical needs of hurting people in our world today.

OTHER TEACHINGS OF JESUS

Right after his baptism, Jesus is tempted to abandon his call to be a suffering Messiah in favor of one who would rely exclusively on his power and status (Matt. 4:1-11; Luke 4:1-13). One of Satan's temptations is for Christ to alleviate his hunger by turning stones into bread. Jesus replies by citing Deuteronomy 8:3, declaring that "people do not live on bread alone, but on every word that comes from the mouth of God" (Matt. 4:4). He similarly refuses to let the angels put on a spectacular life-saving demonstration, rescuing him from a plunge from the temple's portico. He also resists the temptation to worship the devil in return for immediate temporal power over all the world's kingdoms.

SERMON ON THE MOUNT

Jesus' famous Sermon on the Mount (Matt. 5–7; cf. the Sermon on the Plain in Luke 6:20-49) has quite a bit to say about possessions. Jesus draws on the Jewish concept of the *anawim* to bless those who are both spiritually (Matt. 5:3) and materially (Luke 6:20) poor — who recognize that their only hope for physical or spiritual sustenance comes from God. Almsgiving is commended in Matthew 5:42: "Give to the one who asks you, and do not turn away from the one who wants to borrow from you." Early in the fifth century, Augustine wisely observed that Christ did not tell his audience to give exactly everything that everybody asks of you. A beggar's deepest need may not be for a handout that provides him a meal for a day (or tempts him to squander it on something that does not nourish him at all), but for a long-term opportunity to work and provide for himself. But the point remains that God's people care for those in need and work to find appropriate ways to provide for them.

A beggar's deepest need may not be for a handout that provides him a meal for a day.

Similarly, in Luke 6:30 Jesus commands those who make loans not to begrudge their lack of repayment. Against the background of an approaching sabbatical year (recall chapter one), Jewish moneylenders were often reluctant to grant loans to the poor, knowing that the amount that they would receive in repayment would be less than if the sabbatical year was still several years away. Jesus in essence tells them not to calculate the amount of return they will receive when deciding whom and when to help. Matthew 6:1-4 teaches more about almsgiving. Believers should not give in hopes of receiving public acclaim. This is what "giving in secret" and "not letting one's left hand know what one's right hand is doing" mean. Jesus is not telling us to refuse to let anyone else examine our spending for the purpose of keeping us accountable to God's standards. Matthew 6:12 (cf. Luke 11:3) commands Christians to pray for their daily bread. Material needs are as legitimate an issue for prayer as spiritual ones. But, as with Proverbs 30:8-9, we are reminded of how believers today are regularly preoccupied with a far longer-term concern — "annual" or even "multiyear" bread we might call it!

Matthew 6:19-34 echoes several of the themes of Luke 16:1-13 (cf. also Luke 11:34-36; 12:22-34). Jesus warns against storing up unused surplus that merely invites theft or corrosion (Matt. 6:19). One should make "spiritual treasure" a priority, since this will affect one's attitudes about worldly wealth as well (vv. 20-24). Then one will not be consumed with worry about material provisions (vv. 25-34). One verse in this context is often misinterpreted. Verse 33 promises us that if we "seek first his kingdom and his righteousness," then "all these things [food, drink and clothing] will be given" to us as well. Yet thousands of Christians have starved to death throughout church history! The

> Material needs are as legitimate an issue for prayer as spiritual ones.

resolution of this apparent contradiction is not to charge all destitute believers with inadequate faith or obedience, or to so "spiritualize" Jesus' promise that it speaks only of rewards in heaven. Rather we must recall that the entire Sermon on the Mount is addressed to disciples (and would-be disciples) *in community*. The second-person plural pronouns ("y'all," as many Southerners in the U.S. would say) must not be missed. As *the church*, locally and globally, seeks God's righteous standards, she will by definition care for needy fellow Christians, at home and abroad, so that they all have access at least to the basics of food, clothing, and shelter. This principle is even clearer in Mark 10:29-30, when Jesus promises that those who give up possessions for the kingdom will receive back "in this present age" numerous additional relatives (obviously fellow believers) as well as homes and fields (believers' new family members sharing their property with needier Christians).

In Luke 4:16-21, Jesus cites Isaiah 61:1-2a and 58:6 to declare that the time has come to free prisoners, give sight to the blind, release the oppressed, and proclaim good news to the poor. In his ministry, he fulfilled all of these promises in both spiritual and material ways. It is thus reasonable to conclude that he expects his church to do likewise.

TITHES AND TAXES

Luke 11:41-42 and the parallel passage in Matthew 23:23 are the only places in the Gospels where Jesus refers to tithing. In his debates with the Jewish leaders, he rebukes them for tithing down to the most minute spice or crop they produced while neglecting the weightier matters of the Law — the justice and love of God. Jesus concludes, "You should have practiced the latter without leaving the former undone" (Luke 11:42). From this statement, some Christians deduce that they are still required to tithe. But Jesus is addressing his opponents here, not his disciples. And, until Pentecost, they *were* still under the age of the Law and required to tithe. It would seem more fair to say that we simply cannot conclude one way or the other from this passage what Jesus would have thought about requiring his followers to tithe in the new age he was inaugurating.

In Mark 8:36 and parallels, Jesus clearly gives a timeless pronouncement: "What good is it for you to gain the whole world, yet forfeit your soul?" Then In Matthew 17:24-27 he addresses the temple tax. Here he envisions a change from the Old Testament age to the New. The half-shekel tax of Exodus 30:13 will no longer be required for upkeep of the temple, because, as he will later teach, the temple itself will be destroyed (Matt. 24:2). But the principle that he employs here, that the king's citizens should be exempt from paying tribute, may well reflect his attitude to the tithe as well. As long as the Law is in force, tribute is paid so as to cause no offense. But the gospel is not a new Law. It does not legalistically mandate external ritual. Its only absolutes are fundamental moral principles, not outward ceremonies or legislation. Jesus clearly calls his followers to give generously and sacrificially. But for many affluent Christians that probably means much more than 10%!

> Jesus clearly calls his followers to give generously and sacrificially.

RICH YOUNG RULER AND ZACCHEUS

The stories about the rich young ruler (Mark 10:17-31 and parallels) and the conversion of Zaccheus (Luke 19:1-10) occur in close proximity in Luke's Gospel. This is a good hint to suggest that neither model may be absolutized. Jesus recognizes that riches stand in the way of the synagogue ruler entering the kingdom, so he calls on him to give them away to the poor and to come follow him (Mark 10:21; cf. Luke 18:22). But Zaccheus gives away only (!) half, restores fourfold to those he has defrauded and does all this voluntarily, not in response to a command from Christ (Luke 19:8). It is probably not coincidental that Luke next presents the parable of the Pounds (vv. 11-27), in which people can be faithful by making money rather than giving it away. Yet it all reverts to the master, because it ultimately belongs to him. There need be no fixed percentages of how much we spend and how much we give away when we are passionately consumed by the commitment to be good stewards of 100% of our material possessions.

> There need be no fixed percentages of how much we spend and how much we give away when we are passionately consumed by the commitment to be good stewards of 100% of our material possessions.

DEVOTION TO CHRIST

John 12:1-8 and parallels remind us that there is a time and place for costly, lavish devotion to Christ. Mary "wastes" nearly a year's income by pouring expensive perfume to anoint Jesus in preparation for his death and burial. Judas protests (v. 5), but John's Gospel makes it plain that Judas did not care for the poor but was a thief (v. 6). Jesus' closing words have been among the most misused in all of Scripture throughout church history: "You will always have the poor among you, but you will not always have me" (v. 8). This is not an excuse to neglect the poor, merely a reminder that there are exceptional situations in which money may be spent extravagantly in very different ways. The parallel account in Mark confirms this by adding, "and you can help them [the poor] any time you want" (Mark 14:7). Jesus is actually alluding here to Deuteronomy 15:11, which states, "There will always be poor people in the land. Therefore I command you to be open-handed towards those of your people that are poor and needy in your land." In other words, caring for the poor reflects the regular, ongoing commitment of God's people; occasionally funds may be diverted for other purposes. One wonders if most modern, affluent Christians and churches have not exactly reversed these two priorities.

CORRUPTION, PERCENTAGES, AND SACRIFICE

Finally, we must observe Jesus' behavior and teaching in the temple during the last week of his life. Christ condemns the traders and moneychangers for corrupting the purpose of the court of the temple in which they have set up shop — an area designed for visiting Gentiles to worship Yahweh, the one true God (Mark 11:17; cf. John 2:16). He tells the Jewish leaders that they must continue to pay tax to Rome (a separate issue from the temple tax discussed in Matt. 17:24-27), but also to give God his due (Mark 12:13-17 and parallels). He thus avoids the "catch-22" trap set by the Pharisees and Herodians (v. 13), since the Pharisees resented having to pay taxes to Rome while the Herodians supported the practice. Finally, he praises the poor widow who gives two small coins to the

The widow's mite counted for more because it was a higher percentage of what she owned.

temple treasury (Mark 12:41-44 and parallels). In God's eyes, her gift counted for more than the large donations by the rich, precisely because she gave a higher percentage of what she owned — a further clue that in the Christian age there is no one fixed percentage demanded of all believers.

CONCLUSION

The good news of the kingdom that Jesus proclaimed is consistently "holistic." Jesus was concerned with both body and soul. All the charitable deeds in the world prove meaningless if a person is not a true follower of Christ; that individual will still be damned for all eternity. On the other hand, anyone who professes to be a disciple must demonstrate the reality of that profession by transformed living, including in the areas of personal spending and giving. Different people will experience that transformation in different ways and to different extents, but the person who never displays any concern for the Lord's work and for the poor and who never gives anything to help them *by definition* is not someone whom the power of the Spirit has touched. So it is wrong to claim, as some do, that Jesus does not envision any rich Christians. But it is correct to observe that the Gospels never depict a well-to-do person who is a genuine believer and yet who is not simultaneously generous in giving of his or her treasure.

Reflecting on Lesson Four

1. Put in your own words how you understand the balance in the Gospels between Jesus' concern for people's spiritual needs and his compassion for their physical needs.

2. Where today do we see counterparts to the rich fool and the rich man who refused to help Lazarus? Remember that both of these characters from Jesus' parables would have been Jews who believed at the time that they were already rightly related to God.

3. In what ways should Christians today use material possessions more "shrewdly"?

4. What is your attitude toward contemporary Christian giving to the poor? Are there ways we need to give more intelligently? more compassionately?

5. What is currently standing in the way of your having a completely "sold-out" commitment to Jesus Christ and all of the principles of the gospel?

6. In what ways do you unnecessarily worry about finances? How could your church better help you feel free to give generously?

7. What percentage of your income would you honestly say might reflect *sacrificial* giving to the Lord's work, including helping the poor?

Consider this:

Helping those in need has been a foundational activity of the Church of Jesus Christ. It should be one of the most high-profile activities of congregations today. Is it in your congregation? If not, why do you think that is true? How do the dynamics of our society affect the church's involvement in benevolent activities in the community?

5

THE BOOK OF ACTS

In this lesson:

> ▶ Benevolence in the first church in Jerusalem
> ▶ Changing methods as new churches are established
> ▶ The effects of Christianity on the surrounding economy

Some have admitted that Jesus was a "radical," but they argue that the rest of the New Testament "tones him down." That certainly is not true of the earliest church as it develops in the book of Acts, although we will read there about varying models of helping the poor. This reminds us that Christians may take many different approaches, depending on the situation, but in each case they are still called on to demonstrate concern and compassion.

THE EARLIEST MODELS OF GIVING AND CARING

THE COMMON PURSE

Immediately after Peter's first public sermon at Pentecost, the fledgling church in Jerusalem organizes itself around four activities: hearing the teachings of the apostles, fellowship, the breaking of bread, and prayer (Acts 2:42). "Fellowship" (Greek *koinonia*) is explained in vv. 44-45 as involving at least a partial measure of communal living. "All the believers were together and had everything in common. Selling their possessions and goods, they gave to anyone who had need." The practice may be a carryover from the "common purse" that Jesus and the disciples shared (John 12:6). It may have been inspired by the model of the Essenes (see chapter three above). Clearly, certain unique problems faced this new community, not least the fact that many of the first Christians were pilgrims to Rome from around the empire, some of whom decided to stay in Jerusalem rather than go home. How were all these people to be cared for? So we should not be surprised when we later see different models of stewardship of finances elsewhere in Acts.

We must also be careful not to read more into Acts 2:44 than the context permits. Verses 45-46 qualify the apparently absolute statement of the previous verse by explaining how people periodically sold property to meet various needs. Apparently not everyone sold everything as an entrance requirement for joining the church. It is interesting that the clause in verse 45, which could be translated "to each according to his need" combines with one in Acts 11:29 — "from each according to his ability" to form the two halves of Karl Marx's famous Communist manifesto. Marx after all had thoroughly studied Christianity before rejecting

What doomed Marx's ideal to failure was use of coercion and divorcing it from its religious underpinnings.

it. It has been argued that Marx's ideal is indeed Christian and that what doomed it to failure were his means of implementing it: by coercion and legislation rather than voluntary cooperation and by divorcing it from its religious underpinnings. At any rate, if we cannot deduce a timeless, unalterable system for addressing issues of rich and poor from Acts 2, neither should we go to the opposite extreme and call the early Christian "communalism" an ill-advised, failed experiment. Luke as narrator makes it clear that he believes God has approved of and blessed these arrangements (Acts 2:47; 4:33; 5:13-14).

GODLY CONCERNS

In Acts 3:6 Peter responds to a crippled beggar by giving him physical health in the name of Jesus rather than a handout of money. This miracle gives him a forum for preaching his second sermon about coming to Christ. Acts 3 thus teaches two complementary truths. 1) Salvation is always a greater priority than improving one's physical circumstances. 2) But God remains concerned for those circumstances nevertheless. Healing the man's infirmity would have enabled him to work and provide for himself from that day forward rather than rely on the very temporary benefits of small handouts.

TRUTH IN SHARING

Acts 4:32–5:11 returns to the model of early Christian sharing. Luke makes it even clearer here that many of the believers retained private property but simply did not treat it as if they were its sole owners (4:32). As a result, "there were no needy persons among them" (v. 34). Joseph Barnabas is presented as a positive model of someone who sold a field to add to the disciples' treasury (4:36-37), while Ananias and Sapphira appear as a negative model of two who lied about how much they had sold and what percentage of their proceeds they were giving to the church. As a result, both suddenly died (5:1-11).

But why did God seemingly strike them so harshly? It was not because they refused to sell all, but because they lied about what they had sold, and that lie was not merely to other people but to God's Spirit (vv. 1-4,9). Even so,

> Ananias and Sapphira died not because of the amount they gave, but because they lied.

God's people have regularly committed at least as serious sins throughout history without experiencing such severe punishment. A large part of the answer probably has to do with timing. This new Christian community is so young and so small in comparison with the hostile forces surrounding it that nothing short of a high degree of unity and purity will enable it to survive. Interestingly, the Greek verb translated in verse 2 as "kept back" (*nosphizo*) appears only one other place in Scripture, in the Greek translation of the Old Testament in Joshua 7:1, where Achan keeps back for himself part of the forbidden plunder from the conquest of Jericho. In both contexts, a better translation might be to "swindle" or "embezzle." Just as Achan paid with his life at a very vulnerable moment in the history of the Israelites' beginning to occupy the Promised Land, so Ananias and Sapphira pay with theirs at an equally crucial point in the history of the inauguration of God's new covenant in Christ. We should be profoundly grateful God does not regularly intervene in this way. The Bible's teaching about our sin suggests that he would be completely within his rights to do so; it is a marvelous tribute to his grace that he usually withholds such punishment.

INDIGENOUS LEADERSHIP

By the time we reach Acts 6:1-4, some time — perhaps up to two years — has elapsed since Pentecost. The Jerusalem church is now divided linguistically, and perhaps culturally too, between the Greek-speaking Jews from outside Israel who have come to Christ and remained in Jerusalem and the native Aramaic or Hebrew-speaking Jews native to Israel. Because all of the church's first leadership came from the latter community, as needs grow the poor widows within the former community are being neglected in "the daily distribution." This expression probably refers to the gift of either food or money or both. It may well have been modeled on Jewish practices of giving a daily delivery of food to the poorest of the Gentiles within a given town and a weekly ration of finances to the neediest among the native Jewish residents. Wisely, the apostles ask the more Greek wing of the church to select leaders from their own midst to address the problem. They realize they do not have extra time themselves and that God has called them to minister "the word of God," but also that indigenous leadership better understands how to relate to each people group within the church. Because the Greek verb "to wait" (i.e., on tables) in verse 2 is *diakonizo*, the same root from which the noun for "deacon" (*diakonos*) comes, it is usually believed that the apostles here have established the precedent that would later lead to the division of labor among overseers and deacons (1 Tim. 3:1-13) along similar "spiritual" vs. "practical" lines.

SINFUL MANIPULATION

Another negative example of the wrong attitude to money emerges with Simon the Magician in Samaria (Acts 8:18-23). Viewing the apostles' ability to lay hands on people on whom the Spirit came as a power akin to the more occult "magic" that he had performed, he offers to buy this gift. J.B. Phillips's paraphrase of verse 20 is actually more literal than many normally literal translations, as Peter responds, "To hell with you and your money!" Luke includes this episode to warn his readers against any attempt to manipulate God for personal gain.

> Luke includes the episode with Simon to warn his readers against any attempt to manipulate God for personal gain.

KEY PEOPLE WITH POSSESSIONS IN THE EARLY CHURCH

EXAMPLES OF GIVING

As we keep on reading in the book of Acts, several individuals are praised because of their regular ministry of giving to the poor. 1) Tabitha (Dorcas) is eulogized after her death as one "who was always doing good and helping the poor" (9:36). "Doing good" in the Greco-Roman world was often a reference to acting as a patron or benefactor (see chapter three). 2) In 10:2, 4 and 31 Luke describes the centurion Cornelius as a generous almsgiver. His occupation would almost certainly have made him a man of some means. 3) In 11:27-30, the prophet Agabus predicts a famine in Judea, which we know from Josephus was at its height in A.D. 46-47. Under Paul's leadership, the church in Antioch of Syria organizes a collection that is delivered to the elders of Jerusalem, who presumably would then disperse the funds as was appropriate. This is the first mention of the office of elder in the New Testament, probably necessitated by the apostles' moving away from Jerusalem, and it demonstrates that the church continues to vary its model for helping the needy while remaining committed to the principle.

CHANGING ECONOMIC MAKEUP

As time passes and the church expands throughout the Roman empire, becoming increasingly Gentile in makeup, we read of more and more well-to-do Christians. Because of their positions, jobs or situations in life, all of the following people who appear on the pages of Acts would have been at least middle-class and many could have been fairly wealthy: 1) the large number of priests that "became obedient to the faith" (6:7); 2) the family of John Mark, who hosted many Christians in their home (12:12); 3) Sergius Paulus, the Cypriot proconsul (13:6-12); 4) Lydia the businesswoman and head of her household (16:14-15); 5) Jason, who housed Paul and his traveling companions and posted bond to release Paul from arrest (17:5-9); 6) many prominent Greek women in Thessalonica (17:12); 7) the few members of the Areopagus, along with the visiting woman Damaris, who became believers after Paul's "Mars Hill" sermon (17:34); 8) Aquila and Priscilla, tentmakers with the resources to travel extensively

This new religious movement was made up of people from all socioeconomic strata almost immediately from its inception.

(18:2-3); 9) Titius Justus (18:7) and 10) Mnason (21:16). All of these references together do not require us to imagine more than a small minority of the first Christians being particularly well-off financially, but they do remind us that this new religious movement was made up of people from all socioeconomic strata almost immediately from its inception onwards.

CHRISTIANITY'S INTERACTION WITH PAGAN ECONOMIC PRACTICES

CHALLENGING STANDARDS

Six additional passages in Acts demonstrate how becoming a believer not only affected one's personal giving, it also challenged pagan standards in society more broadly. *First,* in 16:17-24 Paul exorcises a Philippian slave girl of her spirit of divination and is mobbed because her owners recognize the loss of income they will suffer from her cure. *Second,* in 17:12 the wealthy Greek women who support Paul and his ministry resemble the women of Luke 8:1-3 who supported Jesus and his followers. In each case, the women function as benefactors or patrons, but without the "strings attached" that normally accompanied Greco-Roman patronage.

ECONOMIC IMPACT ON THE COMMUNITY

Third, 18:3 describes Paul working at his tent-making trade so that he is not dependent on anyone else's support for ministry. Given the reciprocity demanded in ancient patron-client relationships, Paul would accept money for ministry only when it was the case, and clear to everyone else, that no strings were attached that could hinder Paul's ability to freely speak everything God laid on his heart. *Fourth*, Demetrius the silversmith instigates a riot in Ephesus because he realizes Christianity is turning so many people from idolatry that the business of idol-making and worship at the temple of Artemis is suffering (19:23-41). *Fifth*, in similar fashion, so many Ephesians burn their magical papyri scrolls that the value of what is destroyed equals 50,000 days' wages (19:19). Would that the pornography industry in our day would be in danger of going out of business because of Christians abandoning their support of it. Instead, polls tell us that Christians are caught up in it virtually as much as the non-Christian world!

> Polls tell us that Christians are caught up in pornography virtually as much as the non-Christian world.

SALARY CAPS

Sixth, Paul declares as part of his farewell address to the Ephesian elders at Miletus, "I have not coveted anyone's silver or gold or clothing. You yourselves know that these hands of mine have supplied my own needs and the needs of my companions. In everything I did, I showed you that by this kind of hard work we must help the weak, remembering the words the Lord Jesus himself said: 'It is more blessed to give than to receive'" (20:33-35). Instead of endlessly amassing wealth for oneself, the ideal in most of the first-century empire (and in the modern West!), Paul quotes an otherwise unknown saying of Jesus that it is better to give some of one's wealth away.

CONCLUSION

Historically, a straight line can be drawn from the early church's communal life through the daily distribution for the poor by the first "deacons," to the various collections Paul helps organize for the poor around the empire, to the office of deacon as physical care-giver in Philippians 1:1 and 1 Timothy 3:8-13. The models continually changed, but the concern for caring for the poor, and especially poor fellow Christians, remained constant. As Christianity became an empire-wide religion, the numbers of believers with considerable means grew, though probably never beyond a minority within the first-century church. As in the Gospels, most did not sell all that they had. But the first Christians were clearly and consistently *generous* in giving from their wealth and concerned to impact unjust social structures as well as to alleviate personal suffering.

Reflecting on Lesson Five

1. What are some practical ways Christians in modern America could better share their possessions without literally selling off all their property?

2. What mechanism does your church currently have for helping the poor? How successful is it? Can you think of ways to improve it?

3. What projects or programs do you know about that help the poor stand a better chance of being able to provide for themselves in the long term? If any of these are in your community, are there ways in which you could become (more) involved?

4. Who do you think are contemporary equivalents to Simon the Magician, that is, people who try to buy the power of the Holy Spirit?

5. Who are some of the people you know, or know about, whom you most admire because of their generosity in helping the poor? What might you do to become more like them?

6. What other modern social evils besides pornography does the Christian gospel need to challenge? How can believers best go about mounting such challenges?

7. What other ways can Christians today attack the structural evil endemic in our fallen world? You might think about issues related to governments, the business world and educational or legal systems, for examples.

Consider this:

As in the first-century church, the church in the United States today has members from the entire breadth of the socioeconomic spectrum. Do you think modern Americans are more, or less, "class conscious" than Christians in the early church? Does our culture accentuate or lessen instances of discrimination by class within the church? By ethnic background?

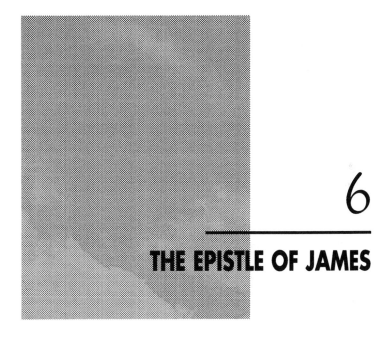

6

THE EPISTLE OF JAMES

In this lesson:

▶ Unacceptable behavior of Christians toward rich and poor brothers
▶ The relationship between true faith and economic status
▶ The fate of rich non-Christians who ignore the plight of the poor

---

The letter from James, the half-brother of Jesus and elder of the church in Jerusalem (cf. Acts 15:13 with vv. 6 and 22), is perhaps the earliest New Testament writing, being penned sometime during the late 40s in the first century A.D. Some writers interpret it as a relatively loose collection of wise

James has a lot to say about poverty and riches.

teachings, something akin to a New Testament book of Proverbs, addressed to Jewish Christians throughout the Roman empire. Others think it is a real letter addressed to specific congregations undergoing socioeconomic oppression. Either way, James has a lot to say about poverty and riches.

PASSAGES THAT ALLOW FOR PEOPLE TO BE BOTH RICH AND CHRISTIAN

WEALTHY CHRISTIANS

Although each passage is disputed, several texts seem to suggest that James believed it was possible for some Christians to be wealthy. 1) In 1:9, James commands believers in humble circumstances "to take pride in their high position," that is, to acknowledge their spiritual status as children of God who will inherit heavenly treasure. Then in verses 10-11, he continues, "But those who are rich should take pride in their low position, because they will pass away like a wild flower," and "the rich will fade away even while they go about their business." Verse 9 explicitly uses the Greek word for "brother" (*adelphos*), while verses 10-11 do not. Thus some commentators think that James is contrasting the poor Christian with the rich non-Christian.

But it seems much more likely that James expects his readers to understand the word "brother" to carry over from verse 9 to verses 10-11. Rich non-Christians cannot take pride in their low position before God; rather that is something they should be

> Material riches count for nothing in God's eyes and will not outlive life in this world.

ashamed of. Instead, just as the poor believers should recognize their spiritual status despite their material poverty, so too James calls on wealthy believers to recognize that material riches count for nothing in God's eyes, that they will not outlive life in this world, and that only an awareness of one's spiritual dependence on God makes a person right with him.

CHRISTIAN ASSEMBLY

2) James 2:1-4 is a second passage that appears to allow for rich Christians. While most first-time readers of this passage probably envision a worship service, so that the rich visitor who is favored over the poor one might well be a non-Christian, a good case can be made for seeing this as an exclusively Christian assembly. The word for "church" (Gk. *ekklesia*) is not used here. Instead James speaks of one who comes into the assembly (NIV "meeting"). The Greek literally reads "synagogue" (*synagoge*), and the language in this context is filled with judicial allusions. Jews regularly tried civil cases in their synagogues rather than taking them to Gentile courts, and Paul will later encourage Christians in Corinth to do the same thing (1 Cor. 6:1-6).

The details of James 2:1-7 support this understanding. Where somebody sat or stood was more significant in a courtroom than in an ordinary worship service (cf. Jas. 2:2-3), and James 2:4 speaks explicitly of "judges with evil thoughts" who discriminate. In the next paragraph, it is clear that James forbids partiality in Christian circles precisely because of the behavior of the non-Christian rich in Gentile courts (vv. 6-7). So we may well be meant to understand James 2:1-4 as condemning the practice of Christians playing favorites and discriminating in favor of rich fellow believers against their poor brothers and sisters in the context of legal disputes. If this interpretation is correct, it would again demonstrate that there were at least a handful of rich Christians in James's churches.

GODLY PLANNING

3) James 4:13-17 is a third text that addresses well-to-do believers. Here James rebukes traveling merchants for planning an entire year or more of their lives without taking God's will into account. Presumably he could not expect unbelievers to make room for God's will unless they first became believers, so that again members of the Christian community are in view. These businesspeople may well be part of the small middle class of the ancient Roman empire rather than truly wealthy, but either way the point is that the early Christians were not uniformly poor. But the "practical atheism" of the behavior of these traders closely parallels the long-term planning of middle-class people, including Christians, in our world today.

Thus while each of these passages seems to prove that James had believers in his churches who were better off than the majority, each text contains an implicit criticism of their behavior that reminds us that affluent Christians have particular obstacles they must overcome. They are tempted to think that their material posses-

> The affluent are tempted to think that their material possessions can replace God.

sions can replace God, that they deserve better treatment than poorer people do, and that life can be secured against all crises.

OTHER PASSAGES DEALING WITH POVERTY AND RICHES

ORPHANS AND WIDOWS

Too frequently in the history of the church, denominations or other subgroups of Christianity have been polarized, debating whether the primary focus of the gospel is other-worldly or this-worldly. One side emphasizes evangelism and preparing people for eternity. The other side stresses social action and the ways God wants to improve people's lot in life right now. James 1:27 reminds us of the Old Testament prophets in refusing to pit these two aspects of Christian teaching against one another. James employs a relatively rare word for "religion" (Gk. *threskeia*) that refers to the outward evidences of an inward faith-commitment. His definition combines together what many have tried to separate: "Religion that God our Father accepts as pure and fault-less is this: to look after orphans and widows in their distress and to keep oneself from being polluted by the world." Without fathers or husbands, "orphans and widows" were particularly marginalized in the ancient world, so the first part of James's definition focuses on social action. Part two balances this out with a call for personal piety and holiness that highlights the spiritual component of the gospel.

POOR CHRISTIANS

Similarly, James 2:5 demonstrates God's "preferential option for the poor," a slogan made famous by Mother Teresa and others who have poured their lives into caring for the most physically destitute of this world. But while Christians should be concerned about all needy people, this verse specifically singles out the poor who are "rich in faith" and who "love" God. God is especially concerned that his people provide for their Christian brothers and sisters in situations of extreme poverty. This verse gives no support to the view that *all* poor people are somehow uniquely blessed irrespective of their spiritual commitments.

FAITH AND WORKS

The epistle of James is best known for its hard-hitting teaching about faith and works. More ink has been spilled since the Protestant Reformation about 2:18-26 than over all the rest of the letter put together. Martin Luther established the pattern by questioning whether James belonged in the canon of Scripture since it appeared to contradict Paul's teaching on salvation by grace through faith alone. Modern scholars of many theological persuasions have agreed that Paul does not contradict James: both recognize that true saving faith will produce tangible fruit (cf. esp. Gal. 5:6).

> More ink has been spilled since the Protestant Reformation about 2:18-26 than over all the rest of the letter put together.

But what is often lost sight of in this discussion is the context in which James's teaching about faith without works being dead emerges. In 2:14-17, James uses the illustration of help for the materially needy fellow Christian as the prime example of whether one performs the kinds of works that demonstrate the genuineness of one's faith. Interestingly, whereas the word "brother" in ancient Greek (and elsewhere in James) regularly functioned generically to include both men and women, here James explicitly adds the Greek word for "sister" (*adelphe*) in verse 15. As with the widows in 1:27, women in general were more likely to be impoverished and outcast in the biblical cultures, but James makes it clear that God does not approve. The Greek also clarifies what remains ambiguous in English translations of verse 14. In the question, "Can such faith [professed belief in one God without any change of behavior, including helping the poor] save them?" the Greek uses an adverb (*me*) that implies a negative answer: "No, such 'faith' is not true saving faith." Put bluntly, if a person claims to be a Christian, is aware of the acute physical needs of desperately poor believers at home or abroad, is in any position to help, but never does a single thing except wish them well, that person's inaction disproves his or her profession of faith.

> If a person claims to be a Christian, is aware of the acute physical needs of desperately poor believers at home or abroad, is in any position to help, but never does a single thing except wish them well, that person's inaction disproves his or her profession of faith.

RICH NON-CHRISTIANS

The final passage on material possessions in this epistle proves even harsher. In 5:1-6 James employs the literary figure of speech known as "apostrophe" to address rhetorically people who are probably not physically present to hear James's letter read as it circulated among his churches. Here he clearly is speaking about the rich non-Christian, and he is equally clearly warning them about the horrifying judgment that awaits them when Christ returns if they do not repent. What is frightening is to observe what is true in our world that was not the case in James's day — numerous, perhaps even a majority of American Christians living "on earth in luxury and self-indulgence" and fattening themselves "in a day of slaughter" (verse 5).

Lest we think this is referring only to the excessively wealthy, we must observe what made the rich landlords' behavior so heinous in this text: they were growing wealthier at the expense of the impoverished day-laborers (we might call them migrant workers in the U.S. or sweat-shop employees in the Two-Thirds World). In America alone, in the last thirty years, the number of poor and homeless has steadily grown, even as the number of upper middle-class and wealthy has skyrocketed. Abroad, even greater inequities abound. For example, in the mid-1990s Michael Jordan earned more money in promoting shoes for Nike™ than did Nike's entire 18,000 person Indonesian workforce that produced those shoes. But unless Western Christians become more informed and refuse to support companies that act like this, they remain unwitting coconspirators in the very crimes James condemned in his day!

> Unless we become more informed and refuse to support exploitive companies, we remain unwitting coconspirators in the very crimes James condemned in his day.

APPROPRIATE CHRISTIAN RESPONSE

In striking contrast, James 5:7-11 outlines an appropriate Christian response. Believers who themselves are financially oppressed by the unjust practices of others can wait patiently because God will soon judge the wicked when Christ returns

(vv. 7-9). But this does not mean they merely pray and do nothing else. They are to take both the prophets and Job as a model of exemplary suffering. Interestingly what James calls attention to about both of these Old Testament models is the way they "spoke in the name of the Lord" (v. 10). The prophets consistently denounced injustice in their day, and they primarily did so within Israel. Job bitterly complained about what seemed to be unfair treatment, and by the end of the book God declared that he, rather than his companions, had spoken rightly (Job 42:8). So while James may have been writing with a side-glance at the Zealot movement, stressing that Christ's followers must not violently revolt to overthrow evil, he is equally distancing himself from the Essenes or other separatist groups that take no social action. God's people should peacefully be at the forefront of movements in every day and age that work for justice for all in this life as well as preparing people spiritually for the next life.

> God's people should peacefully be at the forefront of movements in every day and age that work for justice for all in this life as well as preparing people spiritually for the next life.

CONCLUSION

Once again it goes too far to say that James knows no one who is both rich and Christian. But clearly rich believers must behave in certain ways, recognizing the transience of this life, not seeking any special treatment, and leaving room for God's will to overrule their financial planning. Most of James's churches, however, remain populated by poor agricultural workers who themselves frequently experience discrimination. Together, rich, middle-class, and poor Christians are called on to distribute their resources more equitably and to denounce injustice wherever it appears.

Reflecting on Lesson Six

1. What are the spiritual dangers of being rich that James highlights? What other ones might you add?

2. What are the spiritual benefits of not being rich that James highlights? What other ones might you add?

3. In what ways is it possible to be both rich and Christian in James? Is it equally possible to be both poor and non-Christian? Explain.

4. In what ways does our society discriminate against the poor? In what ways does the church do likewise?

5. What are the closest modern analogies to the situations described in 2:1-7? 4:13-17? 5:1-6? Consider so-called Christian circles as well as other contexts.

6. What might it look like for us genuinely to allow God to overrule our long-range planning, including financial planning?

7. How can Christians effectively denounce and work against social injustice in our world?

Consider this:

On many occasions and in many different circumstances Paul addressed financial concerns within the church. One major concern was motivating the Greek churches to collect money for the impoverished church in Jerusalem. Are you aware of a church in your community which has fallen on hard times? Would our first thought be to find a way to help them out or to hope the members will start coming to our congregation? Suppose a neighboring church building had been burned down by arsonists? Would your congregation be one that would put together a crew to help them rebuild?

7

THE EARLIER LETTERS OF PAUL

In this lesson:
- ▶ Providing for ministers of the gospel
- ▶ Dealing with those who would use their wealth to gain power within the brotherhood
- ▶ Principles for determining the amount which one should give

---

Many Christians who are somewhat familiar with the contents of the New Testament would agree that Jesus and James frequently denounce the sins of materialism. But they would be surprised to learn that Paul addresses the issue of stewardship every bit as much as Christ and the other apostles do. We simply do not pay nearly as much attention to Paul's teaching on this topic as we do to his treatment of other issues. So we will devote two chapters to the epistles of Paul, proceeding through them in chronological order, as best we can determine it. Trained in Jerusalem under the rabbi

Paul addresses the issue of stewardship every bit as much as Christ and the other apostles do.

Gamaliel (Acts 22:3), Paul himself would have been among the top few percent in his society in level of education. A leather-worker by trade and a Roman citizen by birth (Acts 18:3, 22:28), he would have at the very least come from a solid "middle-class" background if not even from the "upper middle-class."

GALATIANS

Early in her history the debate over whether Gentiles becoming Christians had to keep all of the Jewish Law or not threatened to divide the church in two. In an early consultation with the Jerusalem apostles over this issue, Paul achieved a temporary agreement: they did not have to keep the Law (Gal. 2:1-10). What is significant for our topic, however, is that there was never any debate over the need to help the poor. Paul and the Twelve alike were eager to do this (v. 10). In this letter, Paul also exhorts the Galatians that "those who receive instruction in the word must share all good things with their instructor." Like Jesus (cf. Luke 10:7), Paul will break from the Jewish tradition that required professional teachers (rabbis) to be bivocational. Addressing Christian congregations, he will consistently encourage generosity in supporting full-time Christian workers. But he will also forgo this right himself when it is likely to hinder the advance of the gospel (see esp. 1 Cor. 9).

1 AND 2 THESSALONIANS

PAUL'S EXAMPLE OF RESPONSIBILITY

First Thessalonians 2:6 and 9 give an immediate example of this principle. Paul stressed how he plied his trade to avoid burdening the relatively poor Christians in Thessalonica with having to support him financially (on the poverty of the Christians in the province of Macedonia more generally, see 2 Cor. 8:2). In 4:11-12 Paul hints at a problem to which he will devote greater attention in his second letter to the Thessalonians. Some Christians have stopped working (cf. also 5:14). Commentators have often linked this with the Thessalonians' misunderstandings about Christ's return (1 Thess. 4:13; 2 Thess. 2:2); perhaps some thought the end was so imminent that all they needed to do was sit back and wait for it. It is perhaps at least as likely, however, that the problem stemmed from the periodic unemployment that the poorer clients of wealthy patrons regularly experienced (see chapter three). Paul is trying to free his Christian audience from the easily abused "welfare system" of ancient patronage and encourage all to work as much as possible to earn their own keep.

WARNING ABOUT LAZINESS

It is in this light that we must understand 2 Thessalonians 3:6-15, especially verse 10: "For even when we were with you, we gave you this rule: 'Anyone who will not work shall not eat.'" On the other hand, it is important to understand that the

> Paul does not insist that the church care for those who are simply too lazy to work.

Greek in this saying does not use the future tense of the verb "to work" but two separate verbs — "to will" and "to work." A less ambiguous translation would be "Anyone who is not willing to work shall not eat." Then as now, some people eager for jobs simply could not find them, and it is still the church's responsibility to care for them. But Paul does not insist that the church care for those who are simply too lazy to work; indeed he encourages her to disassociate from those people (v. 6).

I Corinthians

MEETING HOUSES

First Corinthians 1:26-29 clearly reminds us that a majority of the first Christians in Corinth, as in most places in the early church, were not well-off. But the fact that "not many" were rich implies that a few were, and it seems that they wielded a disproportionate amount of power in the Corinthian church and caused many of the problems there! Excavations in Corinth demonstrate that the largest meeting places in Corinth were the "villas" of the wealthy that could have held about 30-50 people at a time.

> We must imagine the congregation as a collection of house churches, probably meeting in the homes of the minority of well-to-do believers.

Thus we must imagine the congregation as a collection of house churches, probably meeting in the homes of the minority of well-to-do believers. These new Christians were used to being patrons, complete with all the strings attached to their money in the Greco-Roman system of benefaction.

WEALTH-INDUCED PROBLEMS

The divisions described in chapters 1-4 were probably exacerbated by this segregation of the church into multiple units. The fact that the church had taken no action against an incestuous man (ch. 5) can probably be accounted for only on the assumption that he was one of these wealthy power brokers. The problem of lawsuits (6:1-11) most likely stemmed from the wealthy. Only they sued anyone in the ancient world and then more to increase their honor and status than actual wealth. While prostitution was rampant among all classes of people in Corinth, the well-to-do were particularly able to afford this sin and often had specific "mistresses" on the side frequent their homes (6:12-20).

CLASS TENSIONS

The problem of some Christians not being able to eat meat sacrificed to idols in good conscience (chs. 8-10) no doubt stemmed from the fact that the poorest Corinthians seldom ate meat except at temple festivals as they worshiped a specific god or goddess. The Corinthians' abuse of the Lord's Supper clearly involved the more well-to-do eating and drinking excessively at the expense of the poorer members of their church (11:17-34). This survey of issues Paul has to address does not cover every topic treated in the letter but shows how a considerable number of them may well have involved tensions between rich and poor.

PAUL'S IMPARTIALITY

It is not surprising, then, that in this context, while Paul again defends his right as a full-time Christian worker to be paid adequately (9:1-14), he simultaneously stresses that he has relinquished this right while in Corinth (vv. 15-18). He does not want any rich supporters to think they have the right to tell him what to do or say. He does not even want outsiders to think he is subject to such control even when he is not. Second Corinthians 2:17 alludes to the common Greco-Roman practice of itinerant philosophers and rhetoricians charging audiences large sums of money to

> Paul did not want any rich supporters to think they had the right to tell him what to do or say.

attend their public speeches. Paul attributes this simply to greed and does not want anyone to think he is similarly motivated.

INTRODUCTION OF A COLLECTION

First Corinthians 16:1-4 introduces a topic that will consume much of Paul's attention in his second letter to Corinth — a collection for the still impoverished Christians in and around Jerusalem. Here is the first reference in the New Testament, chronologically, to Christians gathering on the first day of the week (Sunday) rather than on the Jewish Sabbath (Saturday). And part of their weekly worship was to involve an offering. "Passing a collection plate" has formed a part of Christian worship services ever since.

2 CORINTHIANS

RENEWAL OF EAGERNESS

Second Corinthians 8-9 forms the longest, sustained teaching passage in the New Testament on Christian stewardship. Here

Paul returns to his instructions regarding the collection for Jerusalem, applying principles that give guidance for the church's giving in every era of her history. The Corinthians were initially eager to participate but have now lagged behind in fulfilling their pledges. The poorer Macedonian Christians have actually given more in a shorter period of time. So Paul encourages the Corinthians to complete what they started (8:1-11). En route he makes clear that this giving is the voluntary outgrowth of the larger Christian process of sanctification (vv. 4-5). It is a demonstration of the grace of God and of believers' spiritual giftedness (vv. 1,7). And it is the least we can do when we think of how much Jesus gave up in leaving his heavenly home and becoming incarnate and dying for our sakes (v. 9).

> Paul makes clear that giving is the voluntary outgrowth of the larger Christian process of sanctification.

PROPORTIONAL GIVING

Perhaps the most important section of 2 Corinthians 8–9 comes in 8:12-15. Here Paul seems to teach the principle that some have called "the graduated tithe." If ever there were a context in which one would expect a New Testament author to speak about tithing, if Christians were required to give exactly 10% of their income, this would be it. Instead Paul talks about giving "according to your means" (v. 11) and "according to what one has" (v. 12). To what do these expressions refer? Verses 13-15 hint at the answer. Paul is not calling on the more affluent to trade places with the less affluent but wants to create "equality" (vv. 13, 14).

The Greek word used here (*isotes*) could also be translated "that which is fair or equitable." Paul cites the illustration of the Israelites collecting manna in the wilderness. "Equality" for them did not mean that each person collected or consumed the same amount, but that no one had "too much" or "too little." Similarly, Paul does not imagine all Christians having the identical amount of material possessions. But he does recognize that many have unused surplus that qualifies as "too much," while others cannot even meet their basic needs and thus have "too little." To require the poorest of believers in our world today to give ten percent of their income would often just create added hardship for them. To permit affluent believers to give only ten percent would often let them off the hook well before their giving had become truly generous or sacrificial. Thus it seems reasonable to suggest that the implementation of Paul's principles here should call on Christians who earn more than others to give a higher percentage of their income to the Lord's work, including caring for the poor.

> It seems reasonable to suggest that the implementation of Paul's principles should call on Christians who earn more than others to give a higher percentage of their income to the Lord's work, including caring for the poor.

ACCOUNTABILITY IN MANAGEMENT

Second Corinthians 8:16-24 follows this up with an elaborate plan to ensure proper management of the collection Paul is overseeing. Paul is concerned both that all the funds collected actually get to the people for whom they are intended and that mechanisms are built into the collection so that everyone will see that they are managed properly (vv. 20-21). If individual Christians, churches, and parachurch organizations would all find culturally sensitive ways of clearly disclosing the nature of their giving and spending to others within the Christian community to whom they would be accountable, we, too, could curtail substantial mismanagement of funds and suspicion by others of mismanagement even when it has not actually occurred.

REWARD OF A GENEROUS SPIRIT

In 9:1-5, Paul reiterates several of his points about giving generously and without begrudging the gift. Conversely, generous givers must give cheerfully and they will reap abundantly (vv. 6-11). These verses cannot be interpreted as some solicitors claim: send one dollar to a particular ministry and God will send you one hundred in return! Many times the harvest that is reaped from financial generosity is spiritual and not material. But if the church is functioning as she should (recall our comments on Matt. 6:33 and Mark 10:29 in chapter four), believers should feel free to give generously, knowing that, if they ever unwittingly give too much so that they can no longer meet their

> Many times the harvest that is reaped from financial generosity is spiritual and not material.

own needs, other Christians will step in and provide for them. Such behavior would be so countercultural that even outsiders would take notice (2 Cor. 9:12-15). As the light of the world (recall Matt. 5:14), obedient stewardship wins people for Christ as they see our good deeds and praise our Father in heaven (Matt. 5:16).

CONCLUSION

Early in his ministry Paul recognized the importance of Christians helping poorer Christians on a regular, systematic basis. His culture, like ours, contained built-in structures that often hindered this objective. As in the book of Acts, the actual mechanisms for helping the needy varied from place to place and spanned the spectrum from telling them to go to work to taking up an offering for them. But whatever the method, the concern remained. As in James, it was clear too that while there were rich Christians, these believers had unique obstacles to overcome if they were to grow in Christian maturity.

Reflecting on Lesson Seven

1. Is your church generously supporting its paid staff? How would you determine in your culture what would qualify as "generous"?

2. In what situations in our world today might it be important for Christian workers to be bivocational?

3. In what ways do Christians in our society need to work harder to earn more money?

4. In what contexts today do large donors give with inappropriate "strings attached" to their giving? How might this be overcome?

5. What percentage of your income would you have to give away for it to truly qualify as generous and sacrificial?

6. To whom can you disclose your spending practices and learn about theirs, so that each of you can hold the other accountable?

7. How do discussions like this make you feel? Explain.

Consider this:

Humans seem to have a built-in tendency toward greed. How does our society enhance this natural tendency? What does your congregation do to counteract this problem?

8

THE LATER LETTERS OF PAUL

In this lesson:

> ▶ The effects of the patronage system on the church
> ▶ A new perspective on Paul's stringent restrictions on women
> ▶ A family's responsibility in helping needy relatives
> ▶ Warnings against greed

ROMANS

SPIRITUAL DEBT

In most cases, we do not know how the churches to which the apostles wrote responded to the instructions they were given. In the case of Paul's exhorting the Corinthians to more generous and faithful giving, we *do* know: it worked! Paul writes to the Roman church about a year after penning 2 Corinthians, as he is in or near Corinth at that very time. He explains to the Romans that he is on his way to Jerusalem with the funds that he had worked so hard to accumulate (Rom. 15:25). He then adds, "For Macedonia and Achaia were pleased to make a contribution for the poor among the saints in Jerusalem. They were pleased to do it, and indeed they owe it to them" (vv. 26-27a). Achaia is the province in which Corinth was located, so we may conclude that the Corinthians did come through in fine fashion.

In verse 27, Paul introduces a new thought, that the Gentile Christians in Rome owe these Jewish Christians in Judea material support, because the Jews were their spiritual "mother" as it were. Scholars have wondered whether Paul is alluding back to his "olive tree" metaphor of chapter 11: the tree that symbolizes God's people as branches broken off (unbelieving Jews) and wild branches grafted in (believing Gentiles) in order to provoke the Jews to jealousy so that they will again believe. If so, Paul may be hoping that this collection for Jewish Christians will so impress the non-Christian Jews in Jerusalem that many of them will come to faith as well.

CHRISTIAN OBLIGATIONS

Other texts in Romans that deal with material possessions may be treated more briefly. Those whose spiritual gift is giving must exercise it even more generously than the ordinary Christian, who still is called to give generously (12:8). Christians must pay their taxes, even to a godless state like Rome (13:7). They must do everything possible to minimize their financial debts (v. 8). Paul hopes that the Roman Christians will offer him help, including monetary support, so that he can make it as far west as Spain (15:24). Finally, in 16:23 Paul sends greetings from Erastus, Corinth's director of public works. As in Acts, we see here a person who by his office would likely have been quite well-to-do, even if he was the exception among early Christians in that respect.

> Christians must pay their taxes, even to a godless state like Rome.

PHILEMON

This short epistle does not teach directly about stewardship but it does show how Paul was prepared to go to great lengths to see that whatever money Onesimus had cheated his master out of would be repaid, even if Onesimus was no longer in a position to do so (vv. 18-19). Since Paul was apparently under house-arrest in Rome at this point, he may not have had access to large sums of money. Had Philemon tried to take Paul up on his offer, Paul might have had to appeal to those churches (or other benefactors) who from time to time did support him, no small inconvenience under the circumstances.

EPHESIANS

Only one verse in this letter bears directly on our theme, but it is an important one. In 4:28, Paul insists that "those who have been stealing must steal no longer, but must work, doing something useful with their own hands, that they may have something to share with those in need." Paul is drawing on the Old Testament background of numerous laws that required restitution for crimes committed. In our modern penal system, which has largely lost sight of its historic objective of rehabilitation, we have a long way to go to even approximate this more stringent biblical demand for restitution.

PHILIPPIANS

This entire epistle seems to have originated as an extended thank-you letter for financial support Paul has received from the Philippian church while a prisoner in Rome. Despite Paul's comments in 1 Corinthians 9 (see chapter seven), he did not always refuse support from fellow Christians for his ministry. But because of the ancient system of patronage, he makes it clear when he does accept funds that he is not bound to return any favors. Walking this tightrope between seeming ungrateful on the one hand and owing his benefactors something in return explains the language of 4:10-20. Paul keeps weaving back and forth between expressing gratitude for the gift and explaining that he didn't need it because he has learned to be content in all socioeconomic circumstances (see esp. vv. 12-13). God, not Paul, will pay back the Philippians for their support (v. 19). One

One wonders how modern church life might be revolutionized if congregations always sought to recompense their ministers generously while ministers never expected or insisted on a certain standard of living beyond "the basics."

wonders how modern church life might be revolutionized if congregations always sought to recompense their ministers generously while ministers never expected or insisted on a certain standard of living beyond "the basics."

I Timothy

ADMONITIONS ON APPEARANCE

In 1 Timothy 2:9, Paul commands the Ephesian women "to dress modestly, with decency and propriety, not with braided hair or gold or pearls or expensive clothes." The NIV is inaccurate at one point here; the Greek literally reads, "not with braided hair *and* gold or pearls or expensive clothes." There is nothing wrong with braided hair in and of itself. But wealthy Greco-Romans often spent up to one or two hours a day in their coiffure, weaving costly gems into the braids of their hair. Whenever women (or men!) are more preoccupied with their outward appearance than with inward spirituality, they have violated the spirit of Paul's commands here. In fact, this background may shed light on Paul's

> Whenever women (or men!) are more preoccupied with their outward appearance than with inward spirituality, they have violated the spirit of Paul's commands here.

notorious prohibition of women teaching or exercising authority over men in verse 12. Only wealthy women had access to the education in antiquity that would have allowed them to teach men in the first place. If the women who are teaching men in Ephesus are overvaluing their external dress and hairstyle, they are probably distorting God's word in other respects as well, hence Paul's need to silence them.

PROHIBITIONS FOR LOVE OF MONEY

In 1 Timothy 3:3 and 8, under the criteria for church leaders, Paul includes the prohibitions against being lovers of money and pursuing dishonest gain. The terms used are both synonyms for being greedy. Thus we should not be surprised when in Titus 1:11 false teachers are described as seeking dishonest gain, while in 2 Timothy 3:2,4 the terrible people that will arise in the last days are said to be lovers of money and lovers of pleasure.

PROVIDING FOR NEEDY FAMILY MEMBERS

First Timothy 5 contains considerable teaching on stewardship that is often overlooked. While much attention is devoted in Christian churches to the "offices" of overseer and deacon dealt with in chapter 3, the similar "office" of widow in chapter 5 is almost never studied. Widows, as examples of the most dispossessed in Paul's world, who have no family members to care for them and who are too old to work, should be supported by the church (vv. 3-5). On the other hand, working-age relatives have the responsibility to provide for elderly or infirm family members. This is the context of verse 8, which thus says nothing about a man having to be the breadwinner for his nuclear family. (The word "anyone" in verse 8 is simply a generic pronoun referring to men and women alike.) That an adult who refuses to obey this command "has denied the faith and is worse than an unbeliever" does not mean they have lost their salvation, merely that they are acting less nobly than the pagan world around them which uniformly recognized this responsibility to care for needy relatives. Contemporary application can take many forms because of the changes in our society and

> Children have a lifelong responsibility to their parents to see that they are properly taken care of.

the numerous methods available for providing for the elderly, but it does mean that children have a lifelong responsibility to their parents to see that they are properly taken care of.

RESPONSIBLE SUPPORT

First Timothy 5:17-18 includes financial considerations as part of the extra honor that is to be paid to overseers who perform their duties well. Second Timothy hints at this same principle when it declares, "The hard-working farmer should be the first to receive a share of the crops." But again there is a difference between a responsibility that congregations should scrupulously perform and a right that leaders can demand.

CONTENTMENT

The last passages we will treat in our survey of Paul's teaching are 1 Timothy 6:3-10 and 17-19. Here again Paul warns against false teachers and their errant doctrines. Among his description of their character traits, he notes that they "think that godliness is a means to financial gain" (v. 5). Anyone who goes into paid Christian ministry because of the salary that it commands has done so for the worst of reasons. As in Philippians, Paul contrasts this attitude with a contented godliness that is great (spiritual) gain (v. 6). Perhaps echoing Job 1:21, Paul recalls that "we brought nothing into the world, and we can take nothing out of it. But if we have food and clothing, we will be content with that" (vv. 7-8). The desire to get rich leads to many temptations and snares that generate spiritual ruin (v. 9).

Love of Money. Following on from these thoughts comes another one of the Bible's more misquoted and misused texts: "the love of money is a root of all kinds of evil" (v. 10). Paul does not say that "money is the root of all evil" but speaks of "the love of money." Nor does the Greek justify the insertion of the definite article. The love of money is *one*

> The love of money is *one* important root, but not the *only* one, of all kinds of evil.

important root, but not the *only* one, of all kinds of evil. Still, we must not lose the force of Paul's warning. Even translated correctly, as in the NIV, the verse still reminds us of all the ways wealth or its pursuit distracts us from godly priorities in our lives.

Honoring the Source. Thus Paul concludes his letter by commanding "those who are rich in this present world not to be arrogant nor to put their hope in wealth, which is so uncertain, but to put their hope in God" (v. 17). But he balances this with the reminder that God "richly provides us with everything for our enjoyment." Paul is no ascetic, the material world still includes good gifts for God's people, and Christ does not call a majority of his followers to permanently divest themselves of all of their property. Verse 18 explains how we can enjoy a measure of prosperity with a good conscience—when we simultaneously are "rich in good deeds," "generous and willing to share."

CONCLUSION

There is no tension between Paul's teaching about posessions and what we have read in earlier parts of Scripture. As the gospel spread throughout the Greco-Roman world, a growing minority of Christians came from the middle and upper classes of society. Paul never told them to sell all that they had or even to trade places with the poor, but he did regularly command them to be generous in providing for Christian ministry and ministry to the poor in particular. He worked hard to woo people away from the reciprocal obligations inherent in his society's patron-client relationships. He hoped that all might learn what he had experienced — the ability to be content in a wide diversity of socioeconomic situations. And he recognized that none of this was possible without a living, vibrant relationship with the Christ who gives his people the strength and power to live so counterculturally.

Reflecting on Lesson Eight

1. Are there ways in which you have become unnecessarily indebted? What can you do to make repaying your debts a priority?

2. Are you scrupulously honest in reporting all your income and paying all your taxes? Explain.

3. Are there people with whom you have been less than completely upright in your financial dealings? If so, how might you make restitution to them?

4. Irrespective of your actual net worth, are there ways in which your desire for more money or possessions keeps you from doing all God asks you to? If so, how? What can you do to overcome this?

5. Are there people who have helped you financially to whom you need to show more gratitude? Who are they and what can you do?

6. Who are the aged relatives in your family who may need more help from you? How can you best provide it?

7. If you are a generous giver to the poor and to the Lord's work, are there ways in which you are unnecessarily guilt-ridden over enjoying the rest of your possessions? Explain.

Consider this:

We have been examining many references throughout the Bible which teach us God's view of how we should handle our finances and give to the poor. As you have read, you may have seen some ways you could make a change in your lifestyle in order to conform to God's perspective. If not, give that some thought. In preparing for Lesson Nine, be ready to share with others your ideas on changing your lifestyle.

9

THE REST OF THE NEW TESTAMENT AND CONCLUDING OBSERVATIONS

In this lesson:

▶ Delayed rewards for unselfishness
▶ Affluence and charity
▶ Powerful nations condemned for their greed
▶ Stewardship — evidence of a regenerated life
▶ Applying the biblical teachings about money to our lives

HEBREWS–REVELATION

The remaining New Testament epistles and the Book of Revelation add only a little to what we have already studied in our survey of the Bible's teaching on material possessions, but what they include is important.

HEBREWS

This highly theological epistle is written to Jewish Christians, probably in Rome in the early 60s. The author reminds them that, "You sympathised with those in prison and joyfully accepted the confiscation of your property, because you knew that you yourselves had better and lasting possessions" (10:34). Probably the expulsion of Jews from Rome under Caligula in A.D. 49 is in view here. Hebrews 11 presents a long litany of the Old Testament heroes of the faith who never entirely inherited all of the material things they had been promised, because this would not take place until after the Christian era (see esp. vv. 39-40). And in the closing exhortations of the letter, we read, "Keep your lives free from the love of money and be content with what you have" (13:5).

> "Keep your lives free from the love of money and be content with what you have."

FIRST PETER

In his instructions to Christian wives, Peter echoes some of Paul's language in 1 Timothy 2. Women's beauty "should not come from outward adornment, such as braided hair and the wearing of gold jewellery and fine clothes. Instead, it should be that of your inner self, the unfading beauty of a gentle and quiet spirit, which is of great worth in God's sight" (1 Pet. 3:3-4). In his instructions to Christian citizens, Peter echoes some of Romans

13:1-7. First Peter 2:14-25 and 3:13-17 both speak of the need to "do good" in the public sector. This expression was often used in Greco-Roman literature particularly with respect to benefaction. So while Christian giving may have distinctively Christian work as a priority, believers must not neglect other charitable causes altogether. First Peter 5:2, finally, reminds us of Paul's instructions about church leaders, as elders are commanded to serve in a way that demonstrates that they are not "greedy for money."

SECOND PETER AND JUDE

Both of these short letters describe false teachers whose influence Christians should avoid. Among their evil character traits appears "greed" (2 Peter 2:3,14). Second Peter 2:14-15 describes them literally as "well trained in covetousness"! Jude 11 speaks of those who "rushed for profit into Balaam's error," a reference to Numbers 25 and 31:16 in which the pagan prophet who had earlier refused to curse Israel (Num. 22–24) later seduced her into idolatry. In each of these contexts, it is interesting to see how sins of out-of-control spending are combined with references to sexual immorality. Both involve one's inability to delay gratification of one's wants and desires. Fulfilling one's immediate urges is all that counts for such people. It has been said that in our culture, too, one of the best barometers of Christian obedience is how a person uses his or her "wallet and zipper."

It is interesting to see how sins of out-of-control spending are combined with references to sexual immorality.

THE EPISTLES OF JOHN

In his summary of the sins of the "world" — the fallen nature of contemporary humanity — John lists "the cravings of sinful people, the lust of their eyes and the boasting of what they have and do" (1 John 2:16). The New Living Translation captures these thoughts even more powerfully: "the lust for physical pleasure, the lust for everything we see, and pride in our possessions"! To avoid these powerful forces within each of us, we must give from our surplus. First John 3:17-18 puts it quite bluntly: "If anyone of you has material possessions and sees a brother or sister in need but has no pity on them, how can the love of God be in you? Dear children, let us not love with words or tongue but with actions and in truth."

> To avoid these powerful forces within each of us, we must give from our surplus.

Finally, in 3 John 5-8, John praises Gaius for the hospitality he has shown to fellow believers. This would have included providing "bed and board" for traveling Christians, especially missionaries, in a world where public lodging was notoriously unsafe. In an age of spiraling housing costs in many parts of our country, affluent believers can provide significant services to poorer fellow Christians by allowing them to live in their homes with them at a lower rent than the going rate.

THE BOOK OF REVELATION

The final book of Scripture offers encouragement to persecuted Christians in Asia minor at the end of the first century, probably during the reign of the emperor Domitian. John's visions of the horrors of an end-times empire are closely patterned after the Roman world of his day. Just as Christians may have been prevented from entering the trade guilds in the first century because of their pagan religious associations, John envisions a day when believers will not be able to buy and sell wherever they want (Rev. 13:16-18). The prosperity of this powerful empire matches that of first-century Rome. When the empire falls, the list of goods which unbelievers lament not being able to buy any longer reads like a bill of sale to some wealthy Roman in John's world and is composed primarily of luxury items: "cargoes of gold, silver, precious stones and pearls; fine linen, purple, silk and scarlet cloth; every sort of citron wood, and articles of every kind made of ivory, costly wood, bronze, iron and marble; cargoes of cinnamon and spice, of incense, myrrh and frankincense" (Rev. 18:12-13a). But then we read of more common items — of "wine and olive oil, of fine flour and wheat; cattle and sheep; horses and carriages;" and last of all, and most horribly — "slaves — human beings" (v. 13b, literally, "bodies and souls of men")!

As we look for parallels throughout history to this godless end-times world power, we must not be misled by geographic parallels between, say, Russia and "the king of the north" in Daniel 11 or by Iraq and ancient Babylon. The Bible speaks of this empire in language reminiscent of all the godless world powers that people in biblical times had experienced — Egypt, Canaan, Assyria, Babylon,

> The Bible speaks of this empire in language reminiscent of all the godless world powers that people in biblical times had experienced.

Persia, Greece, and Rome, and not all of these occupied the same territory. Scripture is not trying to tell us where this empire will be but what it will be like — an anti-Christian mixture of false religion with great political power (Rev. 17). But Revelation 18 stresses that, like these various biblical empires, it will also be the greatest economic force in the world of its day. Neither Russia nor Iraq comes anywhere close to this today. We must look to the increasingly post-Christian and even anti-Christian Western world, with its powerful governments and multinational corporations, which grows richer with each passing decade as the poorer countries of the world grow even poorer, if we want to find the closest contemporary analogies! Have believers in these rich nations adequately heeded John's call to separate their economic behavior from that of the pagans surrounding them (Rev. 18:4a)? If not, they risk severe judgment (vv.4b-8)!

CONCLUDING SUMMARY AND APPLICATIONS

MAJOR THEMES

Perhaps the five most important conclusions to emerge from this all-too-brief survey of the Bible's teaching on material possessions are as follows:

(1) Material possessions are a good gift from God meant for his people to enjoy. But that means that those of us who have more than others should work to help those who have less to have at least a little more to enjoy.

(2) Material possessions are simultaneously one of the primary means of turning human hearts away from God. It is not impossible to be both rich and Christian, but consistently throughout biblical

> Material possessions are a good gift from God meant for his people to enjoy.

and church history, lower percentages of believers are found among the richer than among the poorer segments of society.

(3) A necessary sign of a life in the process of being redeemed is that of transformation in the area of stewardship. This will look different for every Christian, and it is dangerous to compare or contrast ourselves with anyone else, but over time some noticeable change in this arena will occur if a person is truly being indwelt by the Holy Spirit.

(4) There are certain extremes of wealth and poverty which are in and of themselves intolerable. These vary from person to person and culture to culture but involve, on the one hand, unused and unusable surplus and, on the other hand, the inability to meet even one's basic human needs of adequate food, clothing, shelter, and access to health care.

> There are certain extremes of wealth and poverty which are in and of themselves intolerable.

(5) Above all, the Bible's teaching about material possessions is inextricably intertwined with more "spiritual" matters. No one is ever saved by stewardship; all the charitable giving in the world does not make one right with God if a person does not trust in Jesus as Savior and Lord. On the other hand, someone who never gives to the Lord's work or cares for the poor in any way demonstrates that nothing has ever happened in their lives that could qualify as "regeneration."

APPLICATIONS

The possibilities are enormous and the list of what Christians could do nearly endless. But it may help to list a few practical suggestions that most all readers of this study guide could implement or implement further.

(1) Maintaining a budget helps people to see where their money is going. The more detailed records we keep, the more we can identify purchases that are not truly necessities so as to free up more money for our giving. We must beware of our culture's daily attempts to seduce us through advertising into thinking that luxuries are necessities. Many Christians could easily spend less on housing, cars, recreation, home entertainment centers, telephone and computer-related technologies, heating and cooling their environments, lawncare, and food (recall our comments in the Introduction on eating out) without sacrificing a generally comfortable lifestyle. Most would be surprised how many additional funds would be freed up for Christ and his kingdom.

> Maintaining a budget helps people to see where their money is going.

(2) Avoiding debt wherever possible should be another priority. Most Americans could live most of their lives without ever owing debts on anything besides property and, at times, cars, or schooling. Credit cards should never be used if a person cannot pay the bills interest-free at the end of a month. Those who have already amassed crippling debts should take whatever action is necessary to implement a realistic plan to get out of debt as quickly as possible; Christian financial counselors can help.

(3) The graduated tithe offers an excellent opportunity for those whom God blesses with growing incomes (above the annual cost-of-living increases) to give higher percentages to the Lord's work. A young person or couple just beginning full-time employment can commit to giving 10%, and, without necessari-

ly following any fixed tables, commit to increasing that percentage as their income grows. Others can start wherever they are and commit to similar increases. Churches should model similar practices. If a congregation is not yet giving 10% of its total income in a year to missions, it could begin with that commitment and then pledge to add 1% a year whenever their income increases.

(4) Christians must choose churches to belong to, in part, on the basis of how those churches spend their money. They should look for congregations that give generously to the poor and to outreach at both home and abroad. Because few churches are ever likely to give enough support to these areas to make enough difference in our world,

> Christians must choose churches to belong to, in part, on the basis of how those churches spend their money.

believers should consider giving to individuals and organizations that more directly help the needy on top of their giving to their churches. Groups like World Vision, Food for the Hungry, Compassion International, and others are particularly successful and reputable organizations in this respect.

CONCLUSION

Countless other possibilities remain. But, in closing, it is worth stressing that attitudes are crucial in all this as well. Does working through a study like this leave you resentful of the areas of your life into which it has "pried." If so, it might be good to reflect on all the ways God has been enormously generous with you in your life, above all in providing salvation by grace which we could never have earned. Can we be any less generous in helping others, spiritually and materially? Do you feel a measure of guilt as a result of this study? Some may claim that they are being "manipulated by guilt." If that is the case, then it is important to realize that there is both true guilt and false guilt. If you are already being generous in giving from your surplus, you may need to focus on those portions of Scripture that stress how God gives us material possessions as good gifts for us to enjoy! Relax, put away your false guilt, and delight in God and his goodness. On the other hand, if you realize that there are numerous ways you could free up more money for the Lord and you just haven't been doing it, then guilt is a healthy and biblical motivation. Repent, change your ways, and then you can justifiably "feel good" about yourself!

Reflecting on Lesson Nine

1. How can you focus practically on the joy of eternal life so as to sit more lightly toward earthly possessions?

2. How can you tell in your own life when normal, proper desire for possessions has turned into lust, greed, or covetousness?

3. Who today qualifies as "false teachers," in part because of their unbiblical beliefs about riches?

4. How can you do your shopping so that it does not lead to buying what you didn't plan to, what you don't need, or what you can't afford?

5. What would be some of the easiest purchases you regularly make for you

to forgo or cut back on to free up more money for the Lord's work? What steps toward debt reduction might you take?

6. How might your church address both questions raised above in #5?

7. What individuals or organizations might you support in addition to your local church that are involved in "holistic mission" — meeting needs of people's souls and bodies alike?